CONTEMPORARY TOPICS

Academic Listening and Note-Taking Skills

THIRD EDITION

Helen Solórzano
Laurie Frazier

Michael Rost
SERIES EDITOR

PEARSON
Longman

Contemporary Topics 1
Intermediate
Academic Listening and Note-Taking Skills
Third Edition

Pearson Education, 10 Bank Street, White Plains, NY 10606

Staff credits: The people who made up the *Contemporary Topics 1* team, representing editorial, production, design, and manufacturing, are Rhea Banker, Danielle Belfiore, Dave Dickey, Christine Edmonds, Nancy Flaggman, Dana Klinek, Amy McCormick, Linda Moser, Carlos Rountree, Jennifer Stem, Leigh Stolle, Paula Van Ells, Kenneth Volcjak, and Pat Wosczyk.
Cover design: Rhea Banker
Cover art: © Jennifer Bartlett, detail of *Rhapsody*. Photo: Geoffrey Clements/Corbis.
Text composition: Integra Software Services, Pvt. Ltd.
Text font: Times 11.5/13
Credits: See page 133.

Library of Congress Cataloging-in-Publication Data
Solórzano, Helen.
Contemporary topics 1: academic listening and note-taking skills / Helen Solórzano, Laurie Frazier.—3rd ed.
    p. cm.
 Includes bibliographical references and index.
 ISBN-13: 978-0-13-235570-4 (alk. paper)
 ISBN-10: 0-13-235570-1 (alk. paper)
 1. English language—Textbooks for foreign speakers. 2. English language—Spoken English—Problems, exercises, etc. 3. Note-taking—Problems, exercises, etc. 4. Listening—Problems, exercises, etc.
 I. Frazier, Laurie. II. Title. III. Title: Contemporary topics one.
PE1128.S5949 2009
428.2'4—dc22

2008050495

ISBN-13: 978-0-13-235570-4
ISBN-10: 0-13-235570-1

PEARSON LONGMAN ON THE **WEB**

Pearsonlongman.com offers online resources for teachers and students. Access our Companion Websites, our online catalog, and our local offices around the world.

Visit us at **www.pearsonlongman.com**.

CONTENTS

SCOPE and sequence

UNIT SUBJECT AND TITLE	CORPUS-BASED VOCABULARY		NOTE-TAKING AND LISTENING FOCUS	DISCUSSION STRATEGY	PROJECT
1 **PSYCHOLOGY** **Happiness**	achieve data goal income method	positive psychology relevant requirement research	Lecture topic and organization	■ Agreeing ■ Disagreeing	Taking a strengths survey and applying strengths outside of class
2 **LINGUISTICS** **A Time to Learn**	acquisition environment factor motivation	obvious period role theory	Rhetorical questions	■ Asking for opinions or ideas ■ Asking for clarification or confirmation	Interviewing a language learner and presenting
3 **PUBLIC HEALTH** **Sleep**	aspect consequence function impact	injured link percent shift	Signal phrases	■ Expressing an opinion ■ Paraphrasing	Researching sleep problems and discussing
4 **BUSINESS** **Negotiating for Success**	approach benefits circumstances concentrate	confer conflict resolve technique	Lists	■ Asking for opinions or ideas ■ Expressing an opinion ■ Asking for clarification or confirmation	Role-playing a negotiation
5 **ART HISTORY** **Modern Art**	category communicate create emerged	image style traditional	Definitions	■ Asking for opinions or ideas ■ Agreeing ■ Disagreeing ■ Asking for clarification or confirmation	Researching an abstract painting and presenting
6 **TECHNOLOGY** **Robots**	automatically constructed designed nuclear	obtain significant task	Numbers	■ Offering a fact or example ■ Trying to reach a consensus	Researching a robot and presenting

UNIT SUBJECT AND TITLE	CORPUS-BASED VOCABULARY		NOTE-TAKING AND LISTENING FOCUS	DISCUSSION STRATEGY	PROJECT
7 MEDIA STUDIES Video Games	affects cons evidence grades	interactions issues media pros	Points of view	■ Disagreeing ■ Paraphrasing	Debating about media use
8 BIOLOGY Genetically Modified Food	consume modify normal primarily	purchase retain source	Key terms	■ Offering a fact or example ■ Keeping the discussion on topic ■ Trying to reach a consensus	Taking a food and health survey and discussing
9 ASTRONOMY The Search for Extraterrestrial Intelligence	assume estimate located	project sequence technology	Degrees of certainty	■ Asking for opinions or ideas ■ Expressing an opinion ■ Offering a fact or example	Creating a list of things representing Earth and discussing
10 HISTORY Shackleton	credited depressed finally goal	job survived team	Chronological order (time)	■ Asking for opinions or ideas ■ Expressing an opinion ■ Keeping the discussion on topic	Researching an explorer or adventurer and presenting
11 PHILOSOPHY Ethics	community individual majority overall	philosopher principle unethical	Examples	■ Expressing an opinion ■ Offering a fact or example ■ Keeping the discussion on topic	Writing about an ethical decision and discussing
12 ECONOMICS Opportunity Cost	concepts economics elements excludes focus	fund invest options outcome	Causes and effects	■ Agreeing ■ Disagreeing ■ Keeping the discussion on topic	Role-playing a situation involving opportunity cost

# ACKNOWLEDGMENTS

The series editor, authors, and publisher would like to thank the following consultants, reviewers, and teachers for offering their invaluable insights and suggestions for the third edition of the *Contemporary Topics* series.

Kate Reynolds, *University of Wisconsin-Eau Claire*; Kathie Gerecke, *North Shore Community College*; Jeanne Dunnett, *Central Connecticut State University*; Linda Anderson, *Washington University in St. Louis/Fontbonne University*; Sande Wu, *California State University, Fresno*; Stephanie Landon, *College of the Desert*; Jungsook Kim, *Jeungsang Language School*; Jenny Oh Kim, *Kangnamgu Daechidong*; Stephanie Landon, *Bunker Hill Community College*; Kathie Gerecke, *North Shore Community College*; Patty Heiser, *University of Washington*; Carrie Barnard, *Queens College*; Lori D. Giles, *University of Miami*; Sande Wu, *California State University Fresno*; Kate Reynolds, *University of Wisconsin-Eau Claire*; Nancy H. Centers, *Roger Williams University*; Lyra Riabov, *Southern New Hampshire University*; Jeanne Dunnett, *Central Connecticut State University*; Dr. Steven Gras, *ESL Program, SUNY Plattsburgh*; series consultants Jeanette Clement and Cynthia Lennox, *Duquesne University*

In addition, the authors of *Contemporary Topics 1* would like to thank Michael Rost for his leadership in this project. They would also like to thank Amy McCormick, Leigh Stolle, Andrew Blasky, Jeanette Clement, and Cynthia Lennox for all of their valuable suggestions during development. Last, they would like to thank Jing Fang for his help with their research, and the students from the University of Minnesota and Suffolk University who helped pilot materials from this new edition.

INTRODUCTION

Content-based learning is an exciting and effective way for students to acquire English. The *Contemporary Topics* series provides a fresh content-based approach that helps students develop their listening, note-taking, and discussion skills while studying interesting, relevant topics.

The *Contemporary Topics* series appeals to students in many different contexts because it utilizes a variety of multimedia technologies and caters to a range of learning styles. The *Contemporary Topics* series is ideal for students who are preparing to study in an English-speaking academic environment. It's also suitable for all students who simply wish to experience the richness of a content-based approach.

Each unit centers around a short academic lecture. Realistic preparation activities, focused listening tasks, personalized discussions, challenging tests, and authentic projects enable students to explore each topic deeply.

The lecture topics, drawn from a range of academic disciplines, feature engaging instructors with live student audiences, and take place in authentic lecture hall settings. The multimodal design of each lecture allows for various learning formats, including video- and audio-only presentations, optional text subtitling, optional Presentation Points slide support, and for DVD users, optional pop-up Coaching Tips. In the student book, the 🎧 and 👁 icons indicate that the activity requires either the CD or the DVD.

In order to achieve the goals of content-based instruction, the *Contemporary Topics* series has developed an engaging eight-step learning methodology:

STEP 1: CONNECT *to the* topic *Estimated Time: 10 minutes*

This opening section invites students to activate what they already know about the unit topic by connecting the topic to their personal experiences and beliefs. Typically, students fill out a short survey and compare answers with a partner. The teacher then acts as a facilitator for students to share some of their initial ideas about the topic before they explore it further.

STEP 2: BUILD *your* vocabulary *Estimated Time: 15 minutes*

This section familiarizes students with some of the key content words and phrases used in the lecture. Each lecture contains 10–15 key words from the Academic Word List to ensure that students are exposed to the core vocabulary needed for academic success.

Students read and *listen to* target words and phrases in context, so that they can better prepare for the upcoming lecture. Students then work individually or with a partner to complete exercises to ensure an initial understanding of the target lexis of the unit. A supplementary Interact with Vocabulary! activity enables students to focus on form as they are learning new words and collocations.

STEP 3: F O C U S *your* attention *Estimated Time: 10 minutes*

In this section, students learn strategies for listening actively and taking clear notes. Because a major part of "active listening" involves a readiness to deal with comprehension difficulties, this section provides specific tips to help students direct their attention and gain more control of how they listen.

Tips include using signal words as organization cues, making lists, noting definitions, linking examples to main ideas, identifying causes and effects, and separating points of view. A Try It Out! section, based on a short audio extract, allows students to work on listening and note-taking strategies before they get to the main lecture. Examples of actual notes are also provided in this section to give students concrete "starter models" they can use in the classroom.

STEP 4: L I S T E N *to the* lecture *Estimated Time: 20–30 minutes*

As the central section of each unit, Listen to the Lecture allows for two full listening cycles, one to focus on "top-down listening" strategies (Listen for Main Ideas) and one to focus on "bottom-up listening" strategies (Listen for Details).

In keeping with the principles of content-based instruction, students are provided with several layers of support. In the Before You Listen section, students are guided to activate concepts and vocabulary they have studied earlier in the unit.

The lecture can be viewed in video mode or listened to in audio mode. In video mode, the lecture includes the speaker's Presentation Points and subtitles, for reinforcing comprehension (recommended as a final review). It also includes Coaching Tips on strategies for listening, note-taking, and critical thinking.

STEP 5: T A L K *about the* topic *Estimated Time: 15 minutes*

Here students gain valuable discussion skills as they talk about the content of the lectures. Discussion skills are an important part of academic success, and most students benefit from structured practice with these skills. In this activity, students first listen to a short "model discussion" involving native and non-native speakers, and identify the speaking strategies and gambits that are used. They then attempt to use some of those strategies in their own discussion groups.

The discussion strategies modeled and explained across the twelve units include asking for and sharing opinions and ideas, agreeing and disagreeing, offering facts and examples, asking clarification questions, seeking confirmation, paraphrasing, and managing the discussion.

STEP 6: R E V I E W *your* notes *Estimated Time: 15 minutes*

Using notes for review and discussion is an important study skill that is developed in this section. Research has shown that the value of note-taking for memory building is realized *primarily* when note-takers review their notes and attempt to reconstruct the content.

In this activity, students are guided in reviewing the content of the unit, clarifying concepts, and preparing for the Unit Test. Abbreviated examples of actual notes are provided to help students compare and improve their own note-taking skills.

STEP 7: TAKE *the unit* test   *Estimated Time: 15 minutes*

This activity, Take the Unit Test, completes the study cycle of the unit: preparation for the lecture, listening to the lecture, review of the content, and assessment.

The Unit Test, contained only in the Teacher's Pack, is photocopied and distributed by the teacher, then completed in class, using the accompanying audio CDs. The tests in *Contemporary Topics* are intended to be challenging—to motivate students to learn the material thoroughly. The format features an answer sheet with choices. The question "stem" is provided on audio only.

Test-taking skills include verbatim recall, paraphrasing, inferencing, and synthesizing information from different parts of the lecture.

STEP 8: EXTEND *the* topic   *Estimated Time: 20 minutes minimum*

This final section creates a natural extension of the unit topic to areas that are relevant to students. Students first listen to a supplementary media clip drawn from a variety of interesting genres. Typically students then choose an optional extension activity and prepare a class presentation.

By completing these eight steps, students gain valuable study skills to help them become confident and independent learners. The *Contemporary Topics* learning methodology and supporting multi-media package help students to develop stronger listening, speaking, and note-taking skills and strategies.

A supplementary **Teacher's Pack** (TP) contains Teaching Tips, transcripts, answer keys, and tests. The transcripts include the lectures, the student discussions, the test questions, and audio clips from Focus Your Attention and Extend the Topic. Full transcriptions of the DVD Coaching Tips and Presentation Points are available online at:

www.pearsonlongman.com/contemporarytopics

We hope you will enjoy using this course. While the *Contemporary Topics* series provides an abundance of learning activities and media, the key to making the course work in your classroom is student engagement and commitment. For content-based learning to be effective, students need to become *active* learners. This involves thinking critically, guessing, interacting, offering ideas, collaborating, questioning, and responding. The authors and editors of *Contemporary Topics* have created a rich framework for encouraging students to become active, successful learners. We hope that we have also provided you, the teacher, with tools for becoming an active guide to the students in their learning.

Michael Rost
Series Editor

T O *the* student

The goal of *Contemporary Topics 1* is to help you improve your academic listening and note-taking skills. Using this book will help you increase your vocabulary, improve your listening comprehension, take better notes, and use the information in your notes.

Increase your vocabulary

You will learn vocabulary important to the lecture content, including words from the Academic Word List. This is a list of the most common words used in academic texts. You will hear these words again and again in lectures and textbooks. You will also learn about words that commonly appear together in English.

Improve your listening comprehension

The best way to improve your listening comprehension is to practice listening. Listening will become easier with practice. In this book, you will listen to academic lectures, student discussions about the lecture, and related media clips such as interviews and radio reports. By hearing the same topic discussed in different ways, you will be prepared to listen in a variety of real-world situations.

Take better notes

You use several skills when you take notes. You have to listen to a lecture, understand it, and write down the important information in a very short amount of time. This book will teach you how to recognize the organization of a lecture, and how to use the organization to help you take notes. However, remember that everyone takes notes differently. Try the new techniques presented in this book, but think about what works best for you.

Use the information from the lecture

You will learn to use the information from the lectures in many ways. You will use your notes to answer questions about the lecture and review the information by making outlines, charts, and summaries. You will hear different opinions about the lecture content and then express your own views. Finally, you will take the concepts from the lecture and apply them in new ways during independent projects, discussions, and presentations.

Helen Solórzano
Laurie Frazier

UNIT 1

Happiness

CONNECT *to the* topic

Psychology is the study of the mind and how people behave. One type of psychology is called positive psychology. Positive psychologists study happiness. They try to learn what makes people happy and how people can become happier.

Read the phrases. What do you think is most important for happiness? Number the phrases in order of importance from 1 (most important) to 8 (least important).

____ having a lot of money

____ having a lot of education

____ having religious or other beliefs

____ being good at your job

____ having a lot of free time

____ being young

____ having a lot of friends

____ helping others

Discuss your results in a small group. Use examples from your own experience.

BUILD *your* vocabulary

A. The boldfaced words are from the unit lecture on happiness. Listen to the sentences. Guess the meanings of the boldfaced words. Then match the words with their definitions.

____ 1. If you want to **achieve** good grades in school, you need to study hard.

____ 2. Rosa has several **characteristics** of a good student. For example, she is intelligent, hardworking, and enjoys learning new things.

____ 3. Children have a strong **connection** to their parents. They need their parents and don't want to be separated from them.

     a. a relationship between two things
     b. qualities or features
     c. to succeed at something

____ 4. We gathered **data** about our class. We wrote down everyone's age, gender, and hometown.

____ 5. I set a **goal** for myself: I want to go to graduate school and become a psychologist.

____ 6. I feel a lot of **gratitude** toward my parents. I'm thankful for what they've done for me.

____ 7. Jawad has a good **income**. He has enough money to buy a house and live comfortably.

     a. the feeling of being thankful
     b. money that a person earns
     c. information or facts
     d. something you hope to do in the future

____ 8. To check a child's health, doctors usually **measure** the child's height and weight. They want to make sure the child's size is normal and healthy.

____ 9. One **method** psychologists use to help unhappy people is to talk to them. Another is to give them medicine.

____ 10. You can see a child's **personality** at a young age. Some children are quiet and shy, while others are outgoing and friendly.

     a. a way of doing something
     b. the type of person you are, shown by how you behave, feel, or think
     c. to find out the size, weight, or amount of something

___ 11. I'm getting a degree in math. I don't need to study psychology because it isn't **relevant** to my major.

___ 12. A graduate degree is a **requirement** for becoming a psychology professor. You must have it in order to teach at a university.

___ 13. My professor is doing **research** on the psychology of happiness. She's studying happy people to find out what makes them happy.

___ 14. She has many **strengths** that help her to be a good psychologist. For example, she works well with other people and likes to learn new things.

    a. *something that is needed*
    b. *good qualities of a person*
    c. *the detailed study of a subject in order to learn new facts about it*
    d. *related to a subject*

B. *INTERACT WITH VOCABULARY!* Work with a partner. Notice the boldfaced words. Circle the best word to complete the sentences. Take turns saying the sentences.

1. My sister has a positive **attitude** (with / about) life.

2. I have a strong **connection** (from / to) my family.

3. Psychologists gather **data** (on / in) their patients.

4. My final grade in psychology class will **depend** (on / of) how I do on the final exam.

5. These exercises were **developed** (by / to) our teacher to help us learn.

6. A survey is one method that psychologists use **to find** (on / out) people's opinions.

7. Frank achieved his **goal** (to / of) graduating from college.

8. I feel **gratitude** (with / toward) my teachers.

9. I earn **income** (from / in) a part-time job.

10. Can we change our **level** (in / of) happiness?

11. English is a **requirement** (with / for) my major.

12. Psychologists did **research** (of / on) happiness.

FOCUS *your* attention

LECTURE TOPIC AND ORGANIZATION

At the beginning of a lecture, the speaker introduces the lecture topic. The speaker also often gives a plan for the lecture: the main ideas and how the lecture will be organized. This will help you focus and organize your notes. Here are some common ways to introduce a lecture and the main points of a lecture:

Today . . .

In today's lecture . . .

First . . .

Then . . .

After that, . . .

Finally, . . .

I'd like to . . .

I want to . . .

I'm / We're going to . . .

We'll . . .

get started with . . .

start with . . .

talk about . . .

look at . . .

TRY IT OUT!

A. **Listen to this introduction from a psychology lecture. What topic and main points does the speaker introduce? Fill in the notes below with the words from the box.**

B. **Compare notes with a partner.**

definition	goals	positive	research

Psychology

Today: _____ psychology

1) _____

2) _____

3) _____

LISTEN *to the* lecture

BEFORE YOU LISTEN

You are about to listen to this unit's lecture on happiness. Which statements do you think are true? Check (☑) the true statements.

____ Psychologists can't measure happiness.

____ There is one important way to achieve happiness.

____ People can learn to be happier.

LISTEN FOR MAIN IDEAS

A. Close your book. Listen to the lecture and take notes. Pay attention to the introduction to help you focus on the main ideas and organize your notes.

B. Use your notes. Check (☑) the three characteristics of happy people mentioned in the lecture. Compare answers in a group.

____ 1. They have strong connections to family and friends.

____ 2. They have a lot of education.

____ 3. They are young.

____ 4. They have a lot of money.

____ 5. They have religious or other beliefs.

____ 6. They are married.

____ 7. They set goals for themselves.

LISTEN FOR DETAILS

 A. Close your book. Listen to the lecture again. Add details to your notes and correct any mistakes.

B. Use your notes to decide if the statements below are *T* (true) or *F* (false), according to the lecture. Change the false statements to make them true.

_____ 1. Psychologists measure happiness by interviewing and gathering data on people.

_____ 2. One study found that sixty- to sixty-four-year-olds have the same level of happiness as twenty- to twenty-four-year-olds.

_____ 3. Having religious or other beliefs helps people feel that their lives have meaning.

_____ 4. Happy people set goals that are easy to achieve.

_____ 5. Research shows that people can easily change their personalities.

_____ 6. Positive psychologists develop exercises to help people feel happier.

_____ 7. In the Gratitude Visit, people give a gift to someone they want to thank.

_____ 8. The Gratitude Visit helps people feel more connected to others.

_____ 9. Positive psychologists believe that happiness exercises help people feel a lot happier.

TALK *about the* topic

A. Listen to the students talk about the psychology of happiness. Read each opinion. Then check (☑) who agrees with it. More than one student may agree.

	Mia	Manny	Hannah	River
1. The class is going to be interesting.	☐	☐	☐	☐
2. People can learn to be happier.	☐	☐	☐	☐
3. Happiness exercises probably don't work.	☐	☐	☐	☐

Mia

Manny

Hannah

B. Listen to the discussion again. Listen closely for the comments below. Check (☑) the discussion strategy the student uses.

	Agreeing	Disagreeing
1. **Hannah:** "Yeah, I know what you mean."	☐	☐
2. **River:** "Really? I don't think so."	☐	☐
3. **Manny:** "Yeah, exactly."	☐	☐
4. **Manny:** "I doubt it."	☐	☐
5. **Mia:** "I'm sorry. I don't agree."	☐	☐
6. **Mia:** "I guess so."	☐	☐

River

Discussion Strategy: In a group discussion, you will probably hear **expressions of agreement** such as "Uh-huh," "Right," "Yes!" "I agree." "Exactly!" and "No doubt." Agreeing is a good way to support another speaker and to participate in the discussion.

C. In small groups, discuss one or more of these topics. Try to use the discussion strategies you learned.

- Do you think a person can learn to be happier? Why or why not?
- What can an unhappy person do to become happier?
- What are the most important requirements for being a happy person?

REVIEW *your* notes

Read your notes. Did you write down key words and their meanings? Can you explain the main ideas of the lecture? Work with a partner to discuss and complete these notes.

How psychologists measure happiness:

Characteristics <u>not</u> important for happiness:

Characteristics <u>important</u> for happiness:

How people can learn to be happier:

Now you are ready to take the Unit Test.

Tips!

- Listen closely to the lecturer's introduction.
- Use the main ideas you hear to organize your notes.

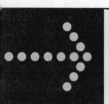

EXTEND *the* topic

You've learned how positive psychologists develop exercises to help people become happier. Now it's your turn to try a happiness exercise!

A. **Listen to a psychology researcher's interview with a grocery store worker who tried a happiness exercise. Then discuss these questions in small groups.**

1. What steps does the man follow to complete the "Using Your Strengths" exercise?

2. How does this exercise make him feel happier?

3. How is this exercise different from the Gratitude Visit?

4. Which exercise do you think will work better to make people feel happier? Why?

B. **To find out about your strengths, take this survey. Read these statements. Then check (☑) your opinion.**

	Strongly disagree	Disagree	Agree	Strongly agree
1. I can easily think of new and different ideas.	☐	☐	☐	☐
2. I am never too busy to help a friend.	☐	☐	☐	☐
3. When I receive a gift, I always thank the person who gave it to me.	☐	☐	☐	☐
4. I love to learn new things.	☐	☐	☐	☐
5. When my friends are unhappy, I try to make them feel better.	☐	☐	☐	☐
6. I like to think of new ways to do things.	☐	☐	☐	☐
7. I love to make other people happy.	☐	☐	☐	☐

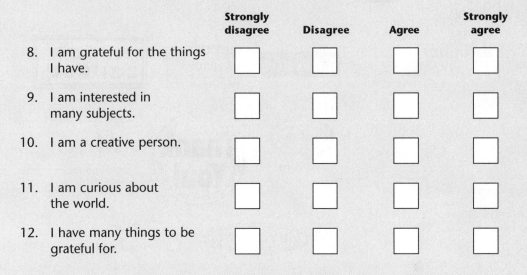

	Strongly disagree	Disagree	Agree	Strongly agree
8. I am grateful for the things I have.	☐	☐	☐	☐
9. I am interested in many subjects.	☐	☐	☐	☐
10. I am a creative person.	☐	☐	☐	☐
11. I am curious about the world.	☐	☐	☐	☐
12. I have many things to be grateful for.	☐	☐	☐	☐

Review your answers. Which statements did you agree or strongly agree with?

Statements you agreed with	Your strength
1, 6, 10	**Creativity:** You are a creative person. You are good at thinking of new ideas and ways to do things.
2, 5, 7	**Kindness:** You are kind and generous. You enjoy helping people.
3, 8, 12	**Gratitude:** You are a grateful person, and you take the time to thank your family and friends.
4, 9, 11	**Curiosity:** You are curious about everything. You like to ask questions, learn things, and explore places.

C.   Try the Using Your Strengths exercise outside of the classroom.

Think of a small task you can do to use your strength. For example, if curiosity is your strength, plan to visit a new place in your town, such as a historical site. If kindness is your strength, plan to do something kind for someone, such as helping a friend with homework. Then complete the task before the next class. Use these questions to help you report on your experience.

┄┄⟩ What is your strength?

┄┄⟩ How did you use your strength?

┄┄⟩ How do you feel now? Do you feel happier? Why or why not?

UNIT 2

A Time to Learn

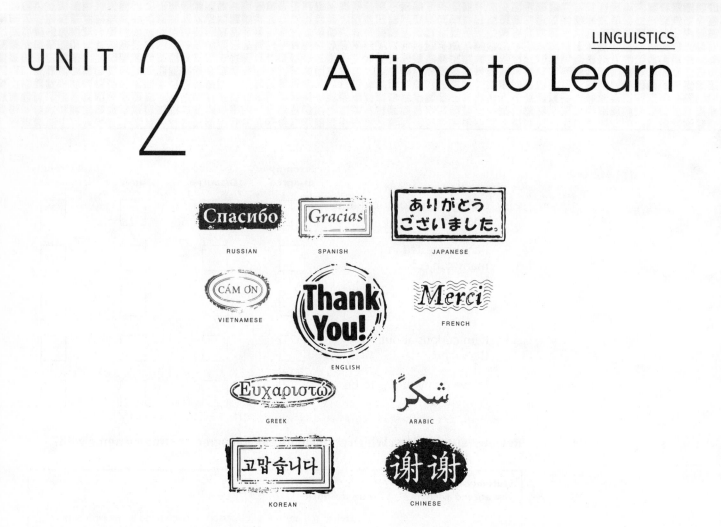

CONNECT *to the* topic

Linguistics is the study of language. One area of linguistics is the study of how people learn language. As babies, we all learned our native language (or languages) from people around us. Many people learn additional languages as children or adults.

Work in a small group. Read the statements. Check (☑) your opinion.

	Strongly disagree	Disagree	Agree	Strongly agree
Children learn new languages easily.	____	____	____	____
Adults can never learn a new language well.	____	____	____	____
A good way to learn a language is to live where it's spoken.	____	____	____	____
Some languages are very difficult to learn.	____	____	____	____
Learning new languages is easy for some people.	____	____	____	____

Share your opinions with the group. Use examples from your experience to explain your opinions.

BUILD *your* vocabulary

A. The boldfaced words are from the unit lecture on language acquisition. Listen to each passage. Then circle the best meaning of the boldfaced word.

There are several different **theories** about how people learn language. But no one really knows how language **acquisition** happens.

1. A **theory** is an explanation of something that _____.

   a. might or might not be correct
   b. is definitely correct
   c. is completely wrong

2. Language **acquisition** is _____ a language.

   a. teaching
   b. speaking
   c. learning

This semester I'm taking an English language class. Next year I'm going to Australia, so I have a lot of **motivation** to study. English is a **critical** skill that I need to learn before my trip.

3. **Motivation** is the _____ you want to do something.

   a. time when
   b. reason that
   c. place where

4. A **critical** skill is a skill that is _____.

   a. easy to learn
   b. very important
   c. not useful

During the first year of life, babies go through a **period** called babbling. During this time, the baby makes sounds but can't say words yet. Linguists think that babbling plays an important **role** in language learning.

5. A **period** is _____.

   a. a length of time
   b. a sound
   c. an age

6. Playing a **role** in language learning means _____ language learning.

   a. having a problem with
   b. giving a reason for
   c. being a part of

Why do so many people study English? There are many **factors** that make it a popular subject. One **obvious** reason is for education. Many students need to study textbooks that are in English.

7. A **factor** is _____ that affects a situation.

   a. the only thing   b. one of several things   c. the most important thing

8. An **obvious** reason is a reason that is _____.

   a. easy to notice   b. hard to understand   c. interesting to know about

---

I think that living in another country is the **ideal** way to learn a new language. You're in an **environment** where you have to speak the language all the time, so your **brain** begins to take in the new language.

9. The **ideal** way to do something is the _____ way to do it.

   a. most complicated   b. most expensive   c. best possible

10. Our **environment** is _____.

   a. how we do things   b. the time needed to get somewhere   c. the conditions around us

11. The **brain** is the part of the body that _____.

   a. controls how you think   b. turns food into energy   c. takes air in

---

B. *INTERACT WITH VOCABULARY!* Work with a partner. Notice the boldfaced words. Reorder the words and write the complete sentence in your notebook. Take turns saying the sentences.

1. Today's lecture is (**acquisition** / **language** / on / **second**).

2. Your thoughts and movements are (**brain** / **by** / **controlled** / **your**).

3. Early childhood is (a / for / **critical** / learning / **time**).

4. In my English class, we're (**an** / **environment** / all-English / **in**).

5. Hard work is (**factor** / important / an / **for** / doing well) at school.

6. The long drive to my parents' house is (the / to listen / **ideal** / to my Spanish language CDs / **time**).

7. Hussein has (English / learning / **motivation** / strong / **for**).

8. One **obvious** (**for** learning / **reason** / a new language / is) to travel.

9. I studied (**for** / **period** / French / **a** / short / **of time**).

10. Parents have (an / **in** / **role** / their children's lives / important).

11. We read an article (about / language learning / **theories** / **on**).

FOCUS *your* attention

RHETORICAL QUESTIONS

A speaker uses a rhetorical question to focus listeners' attention. The speaker does not want an answer to the question. Instead, the speaker uses the rhetorical question to introduce a new point or to signal important information.

When asking a regular question, the speaker usually . . .

> • *stops talking*
> • *looks for raised hands*
> • *calls on someone to give the answer*

When asking a rhetorical question, the speaker often . . .

> • *pauses briefly*
> • *looks at the listeners*
> • *continues speaking*

TRY IT OUT!

A. Listen to this excerpt from a lecture on linguistics. What information does the speaker signal with rhetorical questions? Complete the notes below as you listen.

B. Compare notes with a partner.

Linguistics: Learning Language

1. Babies: How do _____ ?

                     - hear language

                     - ready at birth

            Why do _____ ?

LISTEN *to the* lecture

BEFORE YOU LISTEN

You are about to listen to this unit's lecture on second language acquisition. What do you think is the most important factor for learning a second language? Check (✔) one factor.

____ intelligence   ____ the learning environment

____ a good teacher   ____ other: _____

____ age

LISTEN FOR MAIN IDEAS

A. **Close your book. Listen to the lecture and take notes. Be sure to note the main factors in language learning.**

B. **Use your notes. Choose the best answer, based on the lecture.**

1. The lecturer compares himself to Steven, who is _____.

   a. a six-year-old boy

   b. a sixteen-year-old teenager

   c. a sixty-year-old man

2. The critical period is a time when _____.

   a. a child can learn language very easily

   b. teenagers stop learning language

   c. adults have difficulty learning language

3. The critical period _____.

   a. has a small effect on language learning

   b. is one of several factors in language learning

   c. is the most important factor in language learning

4. Other factors for successful language learning are _____.

   a. teachers, textbooks, and homework

   b. intelligence, personality, and study habits

   c. environment, attitude, and motivation

5. The main point of the lecture is that _____.

   a. adults can't learn a new language

   b. age is not an important factor in language learning

   c. there are several factors that affect language learning

LISTEN FOR DETAILS

What would learning a new language be like for these children? Are they more like Steven or the lecturer?

 A. **Close your book. Listen to the lecture again. Add details to your notes and correct any mistakes.**

B. **Use your notes. Read the statements and check (☑) the correct name, based on the lecture. Some statements may be true for both people.**

	Steven	Lecturer
1. speaks English now		
2. is learning Chinese		
3. recently started studying a new language		
4. is in the critical period for language learning		
5. is in an environment where he hears the new language all the time		
6. could learn better in a different environment		
7. feels embarrassed when he makes mistakes in the new language		
8. wants to learn the new language to talk with his friends		

TALK *about the* topic

A. Listen to the students talk about the critical period theory. Read each comment. Then check (✓) who makes the comment.

	Molly	Rob	Alana	Ayman
1. "The big thing is that it's harder to learn a language if you're an adult, right?"	☐	☐	☐	☐
2. "I came to the United States from Russia as a teenager."	☐	☐	☐	☐
3. "Really? I thought kids learned easily."	☐	☐	☐	☐
4. "To me, the critical period explains a lot."	☐	☐	☐	☐

B. Listen to the discussion again. Listen closely for the comments below. Check (✓) the discussion strategy that the student uses.

	Asking for opinions or ideas	Asking for clarification or confirmation
1. **Rob:** "OK, so what does everyone think about this 'critical period' theory?"	☐	☐
2. **Molly:** "What other factors?"	☐	☐
3. **Rob:** "Really? How so?"	☐	☐
4. **Rob:** "What about you? What was it like for you?"	☐	☐

Discussion Strategy: Everyone appreciates being asked about their thoughts on a subject. **By asking for opinions and ideas**, you can bring up new ideas and help others become involved in the discussion. It's easy to ask, "What do you think?" The next step—listening—is where your learning begins!

C. In small groups, discuss one or more of these topics. Try to use the discussion strategies you have learned.

- In your experience, how does the critical period affect language learning?
- How do factors such as attitude, environment, and motivation affect language learning?
- How can you be a successful language learner?

REVIEW your notes

Read your notes. Did you write down key words and meanings? Can you explain the main ideas? Work with a partner. Discuss the list of terms from the lecture. Then complete these notes.

Term	Def.	How it affects Steven (ex.)	How it affects lecturer (ex.)
critical period			
language learning environment			
attitude about language learning			
motivation for language learning			

Now you are ready to take the Unit Test.

> **Tip!**
>
> Remember: Rhetorical questions are meant to make you think about a topic. You don't need to answer the question aloud.

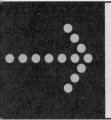

EXTEND *the* topic

You've learned about the factors that affect language learning, including motivation, attitude, and learning environment. Now it's your chance to do your own research.

A. Listen to this audio from a pop-up ad. Then discuss these questions in small groups.

1. What is the businesswoman's motivation for learning a new language?

2. What is her attitude about learning?

3. What is her language learning environment?

4. Is she in the critical period for language learning? Why or why not?

5. How successful do you think she will be at learning a new language? Why?

6. What other factors could affect her language learning?

B. Interview a successful language learner. Use the information below to conduct your interview and give a presentation.

Think of a friend, family member, or acquaintance who successfully learned a new language. Ask him or her about the four factors that affect language learning: age, environment, attitude, and motivation. Use the questions below.

····⟩   How old were you when you learned the language?

····⟩   Where did you learn the language? What was the environment like?

····⟩   How do you feel about speaking the language? How do you feel when you make a mistake?

····⟩   Why did you want to learn the language?

····⟩   Why do you think you are a successful language learner?

Meet in groups of four or five. Make a short presentation about the person you interviewed. Describe the factors that helped the person learn a new language. Then, as a group, compare the people you interviewed. Answer these questions.

····⟩   What similarities and differences can you find among the people you interviewed?

····⟩   Think about the four factors described in the lecture. How did these factors affect the language learners you interviewed?

UNIT 3

Sleep

"This is their idea of a fun vacation."

CONNECT *to the* topic

Public health is the study of the health of people in a community. Public health professionals use education and health services to help people have a healthier lifestyle.

Circle the number of the word that describes how often each sentence applies to you. Then add the numbers to calculate your score.

	Always	Usually	Sometimes	Never
I stay up very late at night.	4	3	2	1
I go to bed as soon as I feel tired.	1	2	3	4
I need an alarm clock to wake up.	4	3	2	1
I feel tired when I wake up.	4	3	2	1
I fall asleep during the day.	4	3	2	1
I get enough sleep most nights.	1	2	3	4
I sleep more on weekends than on weekdays.	4	3	2	1
I wake up feeling rested in the morning.	1	2	3	4

Total _____ = ___ + ___ + ___ + ___

Scoring: **8–16:** You usually get enough sleep.   **25–32:** You definitely need more sleep.

17–24: You should try to get more sleep.

Discuss scores with a classmate.

B U I L D *your* vocabulary

 A. The boldfaced words are from the unit lecture on sleep. Listen to each sentence. Then circle the best meaning of the boldfaced word.

1. Health problems can affect every **aspect** of your life. They can affect your level of happiness, your success in school or at work, and your relationships.

   a. time   b. trouble   c. part

2. Feeling tired in the morning is a **consequence** of going to bed late.

   a. result of an action   b. reason for an action   c. argument in favor of an action

3. I can't **function** if I don't get enough sleep. I have trouble thinking the next day.

   a. work   b. sleep   c. relax

4. Taking the sleeping pills had an **immediate** effect. I fell asleep in ten minutes.

   a. slow   b. instant   c. difficult

5. Staying up late last night had an **impact** on me today. I've been very tired all day.

   a. effect   b. problem   c. source

6. I **injured** myself when I fell down the stairs, and now my foot hurts when I walk.

   a. helped   b. hurt   c. broke

7. There is a **link** between cigarette smoking and cancer: Smoking causes cancer.

   a. cost   b. connection   c. problem

8. Older people are **more likely** than other adults to have sleep problems. They have more trouble falling asleep and wake up more often in the night.

   a. with greater possibility   b. with more trouble   c. with greater difficulty

9. Fifty **percent** of teenagers say they don't sleep enough. That's one out of every two!

   a. a lot of   b. of each hundred   c. a few

10. **I realized** I was tired when I fell asleep on the bus and missed my stop. Before that happened, I'd thought I was getting enough sleep.

    a. thought about how   b. understood   c. forgot

11. My father works the night **shift**, from 11:00 P.M. until 8:00 A.M., and sleeps during the day.

    a. work period   b. vacation   c. day off

12. **Sleep deprivation** is a serious problem—without enough rest, people become sick.

    a. a lot of rest   b. a lack of sleep   c. a short nap

13. I **suffer from** serious headaches. My head hurts for hours, and I can't go to work.

    a. enjoy   b. try   c. am sick with

B. *INTERACT WITH VOCABULARY!* Work with a partner. Student A: Read aloud sentences 1–3 in Column 1. Student B: Listen and complete the sentences in Column 2. Notice the boldfaced words. Switch roles for 4–7.

Column 1	Column 2
1. My grandmother **suffers from** sleep deprivation.	1. My grandmother **suffers** _____ sleep deprivation.
2. It's difficult to function when you have a **lack of sleep**.	2. It's difficult to function when you have a **lack** _____ **sleep**.
3. Sleep deprivation doesn't always have an **immediate effect on** people.	3. Sleep deprivation doesn't always have an **immediate effect** _____ people.
4. Students who **stay up** late may get bad grades.	4. Students who **stay** _____ late may get bad grades.
5. Compared to adults, children are more **likely to** go to sleep early.	5. Compared to adults, children are more **likely** _____ go to sleep early.
6. Many people are **injured in** car accidents each year.	6. Many people are **injured** _____ car accidents each year.
7. Nurses **work in shifts**: days, evenings, or nights.	7. Nurses **work** _____ **shifts**: days, evenings, or nights.

FOCUS *your* attention

SIGNAL PHRASES

Speakers can use signal phrases to introduce a new point, to give an example, or to emphasize an important point. Listening for these phrases can help you understand what is coming next. This will help you better organize your notes.

To introduce a new point:

> Now . . .
> Let's start with . . .
> First, . . .
>
> Next, . . .
> In addition . . .
> Finally, . . .

To give an example:

> One example is . . .
> For example, . . .
> For instance, . . .
>
> This is illustrated . . .
> Let's look at an example . . .

To emphasize a point:

> In fact, . . .
> It's clear that . . .
> Interesting, huh?

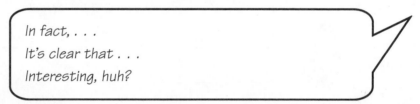

TRY IT OUT!

A. **Listen to this excerpt from a lecture on public health. What phrase(s) does the speaker use to signal important information? Circle the phrase(s) you hear.**

B. **Compare answers with a partner.**

Public Health: Sleep
1. Sleep — children
    more sleep than adults
    e.g. newborn — 16 hrs./day
    Sleep = important!!

Signal Phrases

1. First / Now

2. For example / For instance

3. It's clear that / In fact

LISTEN *to the* lecture

BEFORE YOU LISTEN

You are about to listen to this unit's lecture on the effects of sleep deprivation. Answer the following question.

What happens to you when you don't get enough sleep at night?

_____

LISTEN FOR MAIN IDEAS

A. Close your book. Listen to the lecture and take notes.

B. Use your notes. Circle the five effects of sleep deprivation mentioned in the lecture. Then write them in the two categories below.

car accidents   lower grades in school
divorce and family problems mistakes at work
emotional stress   serious health problems
financial trouble   weight gain

Immediate Effects	**Long-term Effects**
1. _____	4. _____
2. _____	5. _____
3. _____	

LISTEN FOR DETAILS

A. Close your book. Listen to the lecture again. Add details to your notes and correct any mistakes.

B. Use your notes. Choose the best answer, based on the lecture.

1. Sleep deprivation is defined as _____ hours of sleep each night.

   a. needing more than ten

   b. getting less than seven

   c. getting seven to nine

2. _____ of adults suffer from sleep deprivation.

   a. Ten percent

   b. Forty percent

   c. Sixty percent

3. A good night's sleep before a test helps students _____.

   a. remember new information

   b. stay awake in class

   c. finish the test faster

4. Doctors working thirty-hour shifts were _____ more likely to make mistakes.

   a. seven times

   b. seventeen times

   c. seventy times

5. Tired drivers cause _____ of car accidents in the United States.

   a. 10 percent

   b. 50 percent

   c. 20 percent

6. Micro-sleep is defined as a person falling asleep _____.

   a. for several seconds

   b. while driving

   c. at night

7. People who get less sleep are more likely to _____.

   a. eat more

   b. drive more

   c. drink more coffee

8. Women who sleep less than five hours per night are 40 percent more likely to _____.

   a. gain weight

   b. fall into micro-sleep

   c. have heart problems

9. We need more education about sleep deprivation because most people _____.

   a. don't realize that it is dangerous

   b. like staying up late

   c. think they get enough sleep

TALK *about the* topic

A. Listen to the students talk about sleep. Read each statement. Then check (☑) who agrees with it. More than one student may agree.

	Rob	Alana	Ayman	Molly
1. I have a question about the lecture.	☐	☐	☐	☐
2. I learned something new about sleep.	☐	☐	☐	☐

Rob

Alana

B. Listen to the discussion again. Listen closely for the comments below. Check (☑) the discussion strategy that the student uses.

	Expressing an opinion	Paraphrasing
1. **Alana:** "She said seven to nine hours, so eight hours on average."	☐	☐
2. **Ayman:** "So that means it affects the public's health, in other words."	☐	☐
3. **Ayman:** "Oh, good point."	☐	☐
4. **Molly:** "This is really interesting to me."	☐	☐
5. **Ayman:** "That means sleep makes our memories stronger."	☐	☐

Ayman

Molly

> **Discussion Strategy:** In an academic setting, you have many opportunities to **express your opinions**—your thoughts, feelings, and positions. Start expressing your opinions with expressions like "I think" "I believe" and "In my opinion," but make sure to support them with facts, examples, and other forms of support!

C. In small groups, discuss one or more of these topics. Try to use the discussion strategies you have learned.

- Based on your own experience, what are the effects of not getting enough sleep?
- What can people do to get more sleep at night?
- What can governments, schools, and employers do to help people get more sleep?

REVIEW *your* notes

Read your notes. Did you write down key words and phrases? Can you explain the main ideas? Work with a partner. Discuss these points and complete these notes.

def. of sleep deprivation: _____

_____

def. of micro-sleep: _____

_____

	Effects of sleep deprivation . . .	Ex.
. . . on the brain		
. . . at work		
. . . at school		
. . . while driving		
. . . on health		

Now you are ready to take the Unit Test.

> **Tip!**
>
> Be sure you can explain the important ideas from the lecture.

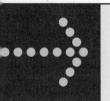

EXTEND *the* topic

Now you know more about sleep and how important it is for good health. To expand your knowledge of sleep-related problems, try the following activities.

 A. Listen to a news interview with a school principal about students and sleep. Then answer these questions in small groups.

   1. What sleep-related problem is described in the news report?

   2. What was the solution to the problem?

   3. Do you think the solution is a good idea? Would you recommend that other schools try this strategy? Why or why not?

B. Research sleep problems. Follow the instructions and then share your research with your classmates.

Choose one of the following sleep problems.

⟶ insomnia   ⟶ snoring

⟶ sleep apnea   ⟶ REM behavior disorder

⟶ narcolepsy   ⟶ hypersomnia (excessive sleepiness)

⟶ restless leg syndrome   ⟶ hypophobia (fear of sleep)

⟶ sleepwalking   ⟶ nightmares

⟶ jet lag   ⟶ night terrors

Research the following questions:

⟶ What is the sleep problem? Who has the problem? How common is it?

⟶ What causes the problem?

⟶ How can you treat the problem?

In a small group, explain the sleep problem to your classmates.

UNIT 4

Negotiating for Success

CONNECT *to the* topic

A negotiation is a discussion between people who are trying to agree on something. Knowing how to negotiate well can help you solve problems with your friends, family, and classmates. Negotiation skills are also important for solving problems in business.

Look at the types of negotiations below. Number them from 1 (easiest) to 6 (most difficult).

_____ A husband and wife are deciding where to go on vacation.

_____ An employee is trying to get a pay raise from her boss.

_____ A country is trying to stop a war with another country.

_____ Two companies are trying to merge (join together).

_____ A student is asking a teacher for more time to do a class assignment.

_____ A teenager is asking to use his parents' car.

Compare answers with a partner. Then share your answers with the class.

BUILD *your* vocabulary

A. The boldfaced words are from the unit lecture on negotiating. Listen to the sentences. Guess the meanings of the boldfaced words. Then match the words with their definitions.

_____ 1. I try to **avoid** having arguments with my coworkers. I change the topic or agree with the person so that we won't argue.

_____ 2. David has a different **approach**. His way of handling problems is to argue that his idea is right.

_____ 3. We need to get along because a comfortable work environment **benefits** everyone. People work better when they get along with each other.

    a. *to prevent something from happening*
    b. *to be useful or helpful to someone*
    c. *a way of dealing with a situation*

_____ 4. My boss **blames** me because the project isn't finished. She says it's my fault.

_____ 5. I don't think she understands the **circumstances**. I need to tell her what happened to delay the project.

_____ 6. Before I talk to my boss, I want to **confer** with my coworker. I want to talk to her to see what she thinks I should do.

    a. *to discuss something with someone before making a decision*
    b. *to think that someone is responsible for something bad*
    c. *the facts or events surrounding a situation*

_____ 7. David and I have a **conflict**. We don't agree on how to finish the work.

_____ 8. We are sewing blue jeans, and I'm worried that there isn't enough **fabric** to finish them.

_____ 9. David wants to use his own **technique** to finish the work. He thinks his way of doing it will work.

    a. *cloth*
    b. *a disagreement*
    c. *a particular way of doing something*

_____ 10. Unfortunately, when I try to talk to him about it, he often **interrupts** me before I can finish what I'm saying.

_____ 11. I hope we can **resolve** this problem soon so we don't continue to have a problem.

_____ 12. We need to **concentrate** on getting the project done. We can't work on anything else until this is finished.

    a. to give all your attention or effort to something
    b. to find a solution to a problem
    c. to stop someone from talking by saying or doing something

---

B. *INTERACT WITH VOCABULARY!* Work with a partner. Notice the boldfaced words. Reorder the words and write the complete sentence in your notebook. Take turns saying the sentences.

1. Different people take (business negotiations / to / **approaches** / different).

2. When two people have different personalities, it is easy (for / **conflicts** / each other / to have / **with** / them).

3. Understanding the personality of the other negotiator can help (**in** / the negotiation process / your **success** / to ensure).

4. A good negotiator is almost always able (**an agreement** / the other person / **with** / **to reach**).

5. Before finishing your negotiations with another company, it's important (**with** / your decision / about / your team members / **to confer**).

6. My coworker is (**concerned** / making / **with** / mostly / a lot of money).

7. I try to (doing / **on** / a good job / **concentrate**).

8. I try to (my coworkers / keep / **with** / a good **working relationship**).

9. I don't like to work late, but I (**to** / my boss / usually / **give in**) when she asks me to stay to finish something.

10. My family **blames** (the long hours / my boss / that I spend at work / **for**).

F O C U S *your* **attention**

LISTS

Speakers often list items during a lecture. For example, a speaker may list the steps in a process. Listen for lists so you can number and write steps or items in your notes. The following phrases are used to introduce a list or items in a list.

> There are (three) things . . .   There are (four) steps . . .
>   The first (thing) is . . .   First, . . .
>   The second (thing) is . . .   After . . .
>   Now . . .
>   Finally, . . .

TRY IT OUT!

A. **Listen to this excerpt from a business lecture. What ideas does the speaker list? Complete the notes as you listen.**

B. **Compare notes with a partner.**

Emotions in Negotiations

How to deal with feelings:

1)

2)

3)

LISTEN *to the* lecture

BEFORE YOU LISTEN

You are about to listen to this unit's lecture on business negotiation. What do you think is the most important goal of a successful negotiation?

a. to keep a good relationship with other businesspeople

b. to find the best solution for your business

c. to find the best solution for everyone

d. other: _____

LISTEN FOR MAIN IDEAS

A. **Close your book. Listen to the lecture and take notes.**

B. **Use your notes. Read these statements. Based on the lecture, correct the errors in the underlined phrases. Write the correct answers.**

1. The lecture describes <u>two approaches</u> to negotiation.

    _____

2. In the "win-win" approach, a negotiator tries to reach a decision that <u>makes the other person happy</u>.

    _____

3. A clothing company and a <u>clothing store</u> are the two sides in the lecturer's example.

    _____

4. The first step in negotiation is to <u>explain your side of the problem</u>.

    _____

5. The next step is to <u>argue for the solution that is best for your company</u>.

    _____

Negotiating can happen anytime people work together.

LISTEN FOR DETAILS

A. Close your book. Listen to the lecture again. Add details to your notes and correct any mistakes.

B. Use your notes. Match each action with the result discussed in the lecture.

Action	Result
_b_ 1. If you learn to negotiate now, . . .	a. you might agree to decisions that are bad for you.
____ 2. If you use a hard approach, . . .	b. your business will benefit over time.
____ 3. If you use a soft approach, . . .	c. you may hurt your relationship with the other person.
____ 4. If you use a "win-win" approach, . . .	d. you can keep a good working relationship with the other person.

____ 5. If you listen and don't interrupt the other person, . . .	e. you may make the other person angry.
____ 6. If you blame the other person, . . .	f. you can find the best solution for both sides.
____ 7. If you explain your problem using "I" statements, . . .	g. you can avoid blaming the other person.
____ 8. If you discuss all the possible solutions, . . .	h. you can hear the other person's side of the problem.

TALK *about the* topic

A. Listen to the students talk about different approaches to business negotiations. Read each opinion. Then check (☑) who agrees with it. More than one student may agree.

	River	Hannah	Mia	Manny
1. I think the "win-win" approach to negotiations is best.	☐	☐	☐	☐
2. I like the "hard" approach.	☐	☐	☐	☐
3. There are a lot of "hard" businesspeople in the world.	☐	☐	☐	☐

B. Listen to the discussion again. Listen closely for the comments below. Check (☑) the discussion strategy that the student uses.

	Asking for opinions or ideas	Expressing an opinion	Asking for clarification or confirmation
1. **Mia:** "Do you guys agree that the 'win-win' approach is best?"	☐	☐	☐
2. **Others:** "Really?" "No?"	☐	☐	☐
3. **Manny:** "You have to think about yourself."	☐	☐	☐
4. **Hannah:** "So you like the hard approach?"	☐	☐	☐
5. **Mia:** "I think you should just keep listening, and don't give in."	☐	☐	☐

> **Discussion Strategy:** To **clarify** means to make something clearer. To **confirm** is to remove doubt. You can clarify or confirm by restating what you understood ("You mean . . . ") or by asking "Do you mean . . . ?" Or you can ask open-ended questions like "What do you mean?" and "Could you clarify . . . ?"

C. In small groups, discuss one or more of these topics. Try to use the discussion strategies you have learned.

- Which approach to negotiation do you think is the best? Why? Do you think different techniques should be used in different situations? Give examples.
- Think about a time when you had a conflict and had to negotiate a solution. How did you solve the problem? Did you use any of the techniques explained in the lecture?

REVIEW your notes

Work in pairs. Use your notes. Discuss these lecture points and complete the notes.

	"Hard" approach	"Soft" approach	"Win-win" approach
Goal of approach			
Problems w/ approach (if any)			

"Win-win" Approach Details

<u>2 main techniques:</u>

1. _____

- when other per. is talking, DO: _____
- when other per. is talking, DON'T: _____

2. _____

- avoid blaming ea. other—how?: _____

Finding solution together—how?: _____

Now you are ready to take the Unit Test.

Tip!

Remember: You can organize a list of information by using numbers.

 # E X T E N D *the* topic

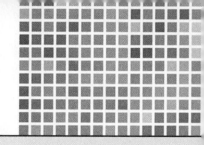

Now you know more about negotiation in business. Try the following activities to expand your understanding of negotiation in business—and beyond!

 A. Listen to this TV ad for negotiation training. Then answer the following questions in small groups.

1. What is the conflict between the two businesspeople? Explain the circumstances.

2. What was wrong with the first negotiation? What made the second negotiation successful

3. Do you think that businesspeople should take courses like this, in win-win negotiation? Why or why not?

B. **Role-play a negotiation. Work with a partner. Create a role-play based on one of the situations below, or choose your own situation. What approach will you use? Will your negotiation be successful or unsuccessful? What arguments will you use? Make notes about your points.**

····⟩ A husband and wife are deciding where to go on vacation. The husband wants to go skiing, and the wife wants to go to the beach.

····⟩ An employee is trying to get a pay raise from his or her boss. The boss needs to save money for the company.

····⟩ A student is asking his or her teacher for more time to do a project. To be fair to the other students, the teacher needs the project to be turned in on time.

····⟩ A teenager is asking to use his or her parents' car to go to a friend's house. The parents need to use the car to go shopping.

C. **Perform the role-play for the class. While you perform your role-play, the other students should listen and answer these questions:**

····⟩ Are the negotiators following a "hard" approach, a "soft" approach, or a "win-win" approach?

····⟩ Is the negotiation successful? Why or why not? If not, what could they do to improve their negotiation?

UNIT 5

Modern Art

Untitled, Kazuo Shiraga

CONNECT *to the* topic

Modern art is the name for art that was created in the recent past. There are many different kinds of modern art. The painting above by Kazuo Shiraga is an example of modern art.

Look at the painting. Check (☑) the adjectives that you think describe the painting. Then add some of your own adjectives.

_____ beautiful	_____ interesting
_____ boring	_____ ugly
_____ colorful	_____ weird
_____ confusing	other: _____
_____ expensive	other: _____
_____ happy	other: _____

Discuss the painting in a small group. Do you like it? Why or why not?

BUILD *your* vocabulary

A. The boldfaced words are from the unit lecture on abstract art. Listen to these descriptions of famous painters. Read along. Then match the words with their definitions.

Kazuo Shiraga (1924–present) is an artist from the Gutai art group, which **emerged** in Japan after World War II. He doesn't paint in the **traditional** way, with a paintbrush. Instead, he **creates** his paintings using his hands and feet. He wants to **communicate** the idea of movement and action in his art.

A museum visitor walks past a painting by the Japanese artist Kazuo Shiraga.

___ 1. emerged	a.	existing for a long time
___ 2. traditional	b.	began to be known
___ 3. creates	c.	to express thoughts and feelings
___ 4. communicate	d.	made something

Leonardo da Vinci (1452–1519) painted one of his most famous paintings, the *Mona Lisa*, in the early 1500s. It shows the **image** of a young woman. The portrait **represents** Lisa Gheradini, the wife of a successful Italian businessman. People like the painting because it is very **realistic**. It shows exactly what she looked like. The painting is most famous for Mona Lisa's smile. From any **viewpoint**—standing in front of the painting or to the side—it looks like Mona Lisa is smiling at you.

A self-portrait by the Italian artist Leonardo da Vinci

___ 5. image	e.	the place you are when looking at something
___ 6. represents	f.	shows something in a particular way
___ 7. realistic	g.	showing things as they are in real life
___ 8. viewpoint	h.	a picture of a person or thing

In the mid-1800s, Claude Monet (1840–1926) helped develop a new **style** of painting called Impressionism. Monet is famous for his outdoor scenes of lakes and the ocean. He also painted pictures of common **objects**, such as fruit and flowers. Other painters in this **category** included Pierre-Auguste Renoir, Edgar Degas, and Mary Cassatt. Impressionist painters didn't mix colors together. Instead, they made small dots of **pure** color.

A photograph of the French artist Claude Monet

____ 9. style

____ 10. objects

____ 11. category

____ 12. pure

i.   a group of things that are similar

j.   things that you can touch or see

k.   not mixed with anything else

l.   the typical way of painting in a particular period of time

B.   INTERACT WITH VOCABULARY! Work with a partner. Notice the boldfaced words. Circle the best word to complete each sentence. Take turns saying the sentences.

1.   The *Mona Lisa* was **created** (by / to) da Vinci in the late 1500s.

2.   A young woman is **represented** (in / to) the painting.

3.   The painting is a (realistic / reality) **portrait**.

4.   You can look at the painting from (different / differently) **viewpoints**.

5.   The Impressionists developed a new **category** (of / to) art.

6.   Impressionist painting **emerged** (under / in) the 1800s.

7.   Impressionist paintings had an important **influence** (in / on) other artists.

8.   Impressionist artists **painted** (with / by) pure colors.

9.   Shiraga's paintings don't show **images** (to / of) objects or people.

10. Shiraga has a different **style of** (paints / painting).

11. Shiraga's paintings communicate **the idea** (to / of) movement.

12. Shiraga does not paint (traditional / tradition) **paintings**.

FOCUS *your* attention

DEFINITIONS

Speakers often give definitions in a lecture. Listen for definitions so that you can write them down in your notes. To signal a definition, speakers often emphasize the term they will define in the following ways:

- by pronouncing the term slowly and carefully
- by spelling the term
- by repeating the term
- by pausing
- by asking a rhetorical question

The following phrases are used to introduce a definition:

> **What** is modern art?   **We say this is** modern art **because** . . .
>
> Modern art **means** . . .   Modern art isn't . . . **Instead, it's** . . .
>
> Modern art **is** . . .   How do we **define the term** modern art?

TRY IT OUT!

A. **Listen to this excerpt from a lecture on art history. What definition does the speaker give? Complete the notes as you listen.**

B. **Compare notes with a partner.**

Art History

Portrait = picture of _____

- painting, _____, or sculpture → shows person's appearance

- all paintings w/ people ≠ portraits

- focus on the _____

LISTEN *to the* lecture

Picasso's *Maria Picasso Lopez, the Artist's Mother*

Picasso's *Portrait of Dora Maar*

Kandinsky's *Contrasting Sounds*

BEFORE YOU LISTEN

You are about to listen to this unit's lecture on abstract art. The three paintings above will be discussed in the lecture. Using these two sentence starters, discuss the paintings with a partner.

- This is a painting of . . .
- I like/don't like this painting because . . .

LISTEN FOR MAIN IDEAS

A. Close your book. Listen to the lecture and take notes.

B. Use your notes. Check (☑) each term that describes the painting, according to the lecture.

	Maria Picasso Lopez, the Artist's Mother	*Portrait of Dora Maar*	*Contrasting Sounds*
Portrait	✔		
Representational	✔		
Realistic			
Abstract			
Cubism			
Non-representational			
Pure abstraction			

C. Match the terms with their definitions.

____ traditional art

____ representational abstract art

____ non-representational abstract art

a. doesn't show an image from the real world and isn't realistic

b. shows an image from the real world but isn't realistic

c. shows an image from the real world and is realistic

LISTEN FOR DETAILS

A. Close your book. Listen to the lecture again. Add details to your notes and correct any mistakes.

B. Use your notes. Mark the statements *T* (true) or *F* (false) according to the lecture. Correct the false statements.

____ 1. Modern art is art that was made during the nineteenth century.

____ 2. Picasso painted the portrait of his mother when he was fifty years old.

____ 3. In the early 1900s, many artists experimented with new types of art.

____ 4. Picasso's *Portrait of Dora Maar* is an example of pure abstraction.

____ 5. Cubism tried to show a person or object from different viewpoints.

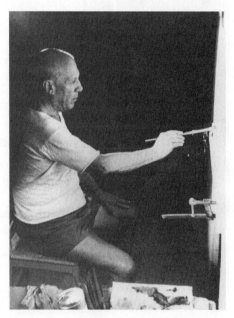

Pablo Picasso

____ 6. Kandinsky painted his first abstract paintings in 1937.

____ 7. Kandinsky used lines, shapes, and colors to represent the way people looked.

____ 8. Kandinsky said that when he looked at a painting, he could hear music.

TALK *about the* topic

A. Listen to the students talk about abstract art. Read each opinion. Then check (☑) who agrees with it. More than one student may agree.

	May	Qiang	Yhinny	Michael
1. I like abstract art.	☐	☐	☐	☐
2. I like traditional art.	☐	☐	☐	☐
3. I don't understand abstract art.	☐	☐	☐	☐

May

Qiang

Yhinny

Michael

B. Listen to the discussion again. Listen closely for the comments below. Check (☑) the discussion strategy that the student uses.

	Asking for opinions or ideas	Agreeing	Disagreeing	Asking for clarification or confirmaton
1. **Yhinny:** "I respect your opinion, but . . . "	☐	☐	☐	☐
2. **Qiang:** "I'm like you . . . "	☐	☐	☐	☐
3. **May:** "Was it a cubist piece of work? Was it modern art?"	☐	☐	☐	☐
4. **Michael:** "Well, what do you guys think?"	☐	☐	☐	☐
5. **May:** "Oh, yeah."	☐	☐	☐	☐
6. **May:** "Is that strange?"	☐	☐	☐	☐

> **Discussion Strategy:** In most conversations, it is important to **express disagreement** without being rude. One way to do this is to first acknowledge the other person's point: "I see what you're saying, but . . . " You can also be more direct: "I simply disagree." Some people soften their disagreement with an apology: "I'm sorry, but . . . " And of course, body language and tone can also make your message more polite.

C. In small groups, discuss one or more of these topics. Try to use the discussion strategies you have learned.

- Which of the three paintings discussed in the lecture do you like most? Why?
- What type of art do you prefer—traditional art or modern art? Why?

REVIEW *your* notes

Work with a partner. Discuss the meanings of the following terms, using examples from the lecture. Then complete these notes.

Term	Def.	Ex.
traditional art	the style of art made before 1900	the portrait of Picasso's mother
modern art		
representational		
realistic		
abstract		
cubism		
non-representational		
pure abstraction		

Now you are ready to take the Unit Test.

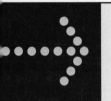

EXTEND *the* topic

You've learned a bit about modern art. Now try expanding your understanding of abstract art with the following activities.

 A. Listen to this interview with an art museum guide. Then check (☑) the three suggestions that the guide makes for looking at abstract art. Compare answers with your classmates.

_____ 1. Learn about the history of the painting.

_____ 2. Look at the painting from different viewpoints.

_____ 3. Think about how the painting makes you feel.

_____ 4. Choose the paintings you like best.

_____ 5. Notice the colors and shapes that the artist used.

_____ 6. Relax and enjoy the painting.

B. Discuss the following questions with a partner.

   1.   Do you enjoy looking at abstract art? Why or why not?

   2.   What is the most memorable piece of art you have ever seen?
        Why did you like it?

**C. Now research an abstract painting by a painter not discussed in the lecture
and do the following:**

····⟩ Find a picture and bring it to class.

····⟩ Go online or to the library to research the painting and the painter. Find
        and complete the information below.

Name of painting: _____

Year painted: _____

Painter's name: _____

Nationality: _____

Dates of birth/death: _____

Style of painting: _____

What the painting expresses or represents: _____

_____

How the painting was made: _____

Other interesting information: _____

_____

In a small group, put your pictures on the wall, like in an art gallery. Stand
next to your paintings. Present the information about your paintings to your
classmates.

When another group has posted its pictures, walk around the room and look
at all of the paintings. Listen to your classmates talk about the paintings,
and ask questions.

UNIT 6

Robots

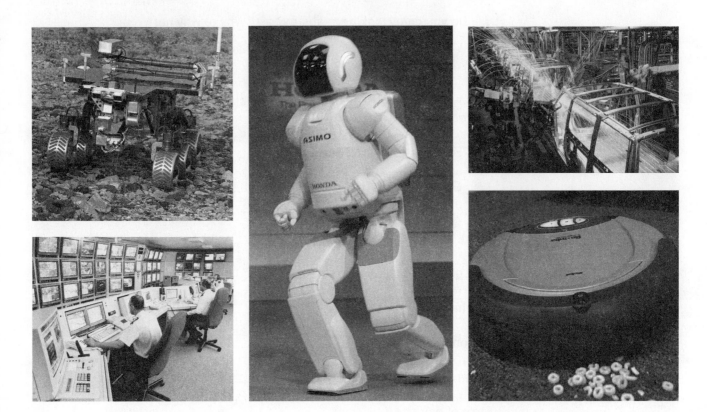

CONNECT *to the* **topic**

A robot is a machine that can move by itself. The Czechoslovakian writer Karel Capek introduced the word robot *in 1921. The word comes from the Czech word* robota, *which means "forced labor." Today, scientists in the field of robotics develop robots to do many different kinds of work.*

What kinds of jobs or work can robots do? What *can't* robots do? Make two lists.

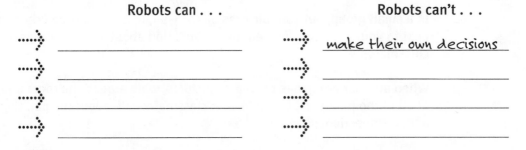

Robots can . . .	Robots can't . . .
┄┄⟩ _____	┄┄⟩ *make their own decisions*
┄┄⟩ _____	┄┄⟩ _____
┄┄⟩ _____	┄┄⟩ _____
┄┄⟩ _____	┄┄⟩ _____

Share your lists with the class.

BUILD *your* vocabulary

Workers along an assembly line at a Ford Motor Company factory

A. **The boldfaced words are from the unit lecture on robots. Listen to the passages. Read along. Then match the words with their definitions.**

In 1769, French inventor Nicolas Cugnot **designed** the first automobile. This **mechanical** vehicle was powered by steam. Using Cugnot's drawings, a mechanic named M. Brezin **constructed** the automobile. It was large enough to carry four people and heavy weapons.

In 1885, German engineer Gottlieb Daimler designed the first gas engine. Soon after that, other carmakers began to make and sell gas-powered cars for personal use.

Then, in 1913, American businessman Henry Ford created the first moving assembly line in his car factory. As the car moved along the assembly line, each worker performed only one **task**, such as attaching a single part. The assembly line had a big impact on **industry** because companies could produce goods more quickly and cheaply. However, many people say that work on an assembly line is very **dull** because workers repeat the same task over and over again.

___ 1. designed	a.	a piece of work to be done
___ 2. mechanical	b.	boring
___ 3. constructed	c.	machine-like
___ 4. task	d.	made the plans for
___ 5. industry	e.	business
___ 6. dull	f.	built

In the 1980s, scientists created the first robotic cars. A robotic car can move **automatically**, without a driver. Scientists have also created airplanes that are controlled by a computer and **programmed** to fly without a pilot. These aircraft have been used to **explore** hard-to-reach places. They can take pictures and **obtain** information about these places.

Recently, scientists have begun to develop robotic aircraft that are powered by **nuclear** energy. These powerful aircraft would be able to stay in the air for months at a time.

In the future, robotic vehicles could have a **significant** impact on travel, exploration, and warfare.

___	7. automatically	g.	to find out about a place by traveling through it
___	8. programmed		
___	9. explore	h.	important
___	10. obtain	i.	by itself
___	11. nuclear	j.	instructed by a computer to do something
___	12. significant	k.	energy from a divided atom
		l.	to get

B. *INTERACT WITH VOCABULARY!* Work in pairs. Student A: Read aloud sentence starters 1–5 from Column 1. Student B: Listen and complete each sentence with a phrase from Column 2. Notice the boldfaced words. Switch roles for 6–10.

Column 1	Column 2
1. The first automobile was **designed**	a. **by** steam.
2. It was **powered**	b. **in** industry.
3. Henry Ford was the **creator**	c. **by** different workers.
4. Assembly lines are **used**	d. **by** Joseph Cugnot.
5. In a factory, different tasks are **performed**	e. **of** the first assembly line.

6. Robots can **pick**	f. **for** city driving.
7. Robots are **significant**	g. **by** these robotic airplanes.
8. Some robotic cars are **programmed**	h. **up** things without getting tired.
9. Robotic airplanes can **get information**	i. **from** hard-to-reach places.
10. Even detailed photos can be **obtained**	j. **to** the success of industry.

FOCUS *your* attention

NUMBERS

Speakers often use numbers in a lecture. It's important to understand the numbers and to write them down correctly. Understanding syllable stress can help you to hear the difference between similar numbers:

- Numbers ending in *-teen* have stress on the second syllable: 13 = *thirTEEN*.
- Numbers ending in *-ty* have stress on the first syllable: 30 = *THIRty*.

Listening for numbers such as *hundred*, *thousand*, and *million* can help you to hear large numbers.

1,200	*one thousand two hundred or twelve hundred*
32,000	*thirty-two thousand*
1,000,000	*one million*

And years.

500 BCE (before common era)	*five hundred BCE*
1769	*seventeen sixty-nine*
the 1960s	*the nineteen sixties*
2003	*two thousand three*

TRY IT OUT!

A. Listen to this excerpt from a lecture on robotics. Complete the notes below.

B. Compare notes with a partner.

Beginning _____ – robotic car competition: all cars = robots

_____ – cars raced: _____ miles, _____ teams, $_____ prize

1st place: _____ mph, finished _____ min. before 2nd place car

LISTEN *to the* lecture

BEFORE YOU LISTEN

You are about to listen to this unit's lecture on robots. What do you know about robots? Answer these questions.

1. When do you think the first robot was constructed?

   a. 400 BCE   b. 1898   c. 1954

2. What are the most common uses of robots?

   a. in industry   b. for exploring   c. for personal use

LISTEN FOR MAIN IDEAS

A. Close your book. Listen to the lecture and take notes.

B. Use your notes. Number the pictures 1 to 6 in the order they are discussed in the lecture.

_____ exploring robot

_____ Tesla's radio-controlled boat

_____ industrial robot

_____ da Vinci's robot sketch

_____ personal robot

_____ Archytas, creator of a mechanical bird

LISTEN FOR DETAILS

A. Close your book. Listen to the lecture again. Add details to your notes and correct any mistakes.

B. Use your notes to complete the statements below, according to the lecture. Circle *a*, *b*, or *c*.

1. Archytas built his mechanical pigeon about _____.

   a. 1,400 years ago   b. 2,400 years ago   c. 1,400 BCE

2. The knight designed by Leonardo da Vinci was able to _____ like a human.

   a. talk   b. move   c. fight

3. Nikola Tesla constructed the first _____ robot.

   a. programmable   b. radio-controlled   c. steam-powered

4. Computers were first developed in the late _____.

   a. 1940s   b. 1950s   c. 1960s

5. In 1954, George Devol created the first robot that was controlled by _____.

   a. a computer   b. a radio   c. a battery

6. Today, robots must be able to obtain information from their environment and _____.

   a. pick up objects   b. taste things   c. perform a task

7. The "3 Ds" describe work that is dull, _____.

   a. detailed, and deadly   b. dirty, and dangerous   c. dirty, and difficult

8. Of all the robots used today, _____ are in factories.

   a. 90 percent   b. 19 percent   c. 90,000

9. Robots are used to explore _____.

   a. the sun   b. the desert   c. volcanoes

10. In 2004, about _____ personal robots were used in the world.

    a. 2 million   b. 2 billion   c. 200 million

TALK *about the* topic

A. Listen to the students talk about robots. Read each opinion. Then check (☑) who agrees with it. More than one student may agree.

	Alana	Rob	Molly	Ayman
1. It's interesting that robots have "senses."	☐	☐	☐	☐
2. I don't think robots should be used to care for sick or old people.	☐	☐	☐	☐
3. I would like to have my own robot.	☐	☐	☐	☐

Alana

Rob

Molly

Ayman

B. Listen to the discussion again. Listen closely for the comments below. Check (☑) the discussion strategy that the student uses.

	Offering a fact or example	Trying to reach a consensus
1. **Alana:** "There are a lot of different kinds of robots . . . like those in factories."	☐	☐
2. **Ayman:** "And we learned that a robot has to have senses—you know, like it can feel, even smell, or see."	☐	☐
3. **Alana:** "They have to be able to do a job, like pick something up and move it."	☐	☐
4. **Molly:** "So, anything else? Great. Well, that's our basic definition!"	☐	☐
5. **Rob:** "Do you want to move on to talk about the idea of robots for personal use?"	☐	☐

> **Discussion Strategy:** By **offering a fact or example**, you can support your opinion and add new information on a topic. This can make the topic more understandable and more memorable. Personal experiences ("In my experience . . . "), observations ("I've noticed . . . "), and media ("I just read this article in the *Times* . . . ") are a few ways you can begin.

C. In small groups, discuss one or more of these topics. Try to use the discussion strategies you have learned.

- Would you like to have a personal robot? If so, what would you like it to do?
- What do you think about using robots to perform tasks such as caring for sick people?
- How can robots make our lives better? What dangers could robots create?

REVIEW *your* **notes**

Work with a partner. Use your notes. Discuss these points from the lecture and complete the notes below.

<u>def. of robot:</u>

    <u>2 things a robot must be able to do:</u>
    1)
    2)

<u>types of tasks + ex.:</u>

dull:

dirty:

dangerous:

	Created in:	Use/ability:
Archytas's "pigeon"		could fly — not far
da Vinci's knight	1495	
Tesla's boat		
Industrial robot		
Exploring robot		
Personal robot		

Now you are ready to take the Unit Test.

Tip!

Remember: Using *K* for thousands and *M* for million are two quick ways to note long numbers.

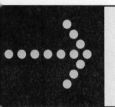

EXTEND *the* topic

You've learned about personal robots that are used by people in their homes. See what more you can learn by doing the following activities.

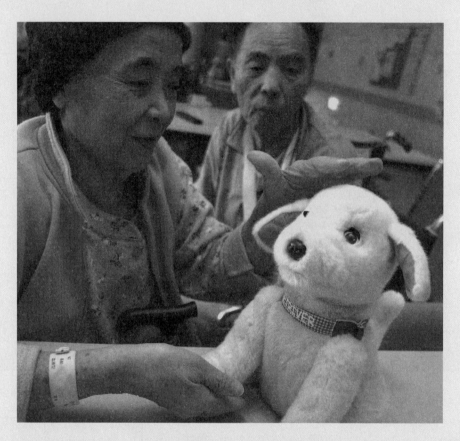

 A. Listen to this news report about a new kind of pet, a robotic dog. Then put a check (☑) in the box if the statement is true for that group.

	Sparky group	AIBO group
1. The people were old and lived alone.		
2. The people were visited by a real dog.		
3. The people were visited by a robotic dog.		
4. The dog visited every week, wagged its tail, and let the people pet it.		
5. The people felt happier and less lonely.		

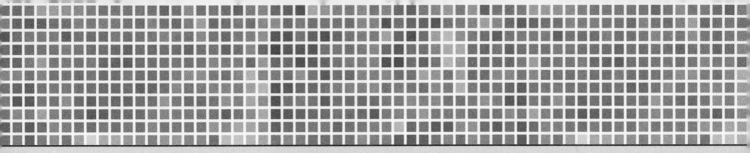

B. **Discuss the following questions with a partner.**

1. Why do you think the people in both groups felt happier?

2. Do you think robots can be good companions for people? Why or why not?

C. **Research a robot. Go online or to the library to research a robot not discussed in the lecture. Find out the following information.**

⟶ Who designed the robot?

⟶ When and where was it constructed?

⟶ What does it look like?

⟶ What senses does the robot have? In other words, can it see, feel, hear, taste, or smell?

⟶ What tasks can it perform?

⟶ Where is the robot used?

D. **Present your robot to the class. If possible, show a picture of the robot.**

E. **Vote for your favorite robots. Respond to these questions.**

⟶ Which robot is most interesting?

⟶ Which one is most useful?

⟶ Which one would you most like to have?

UNIT 7

Video Games

CONNECT *to the* topic

Every day we use a variety of media—books, newspapers, television, blogs, e-mail, radio. A relatively new kind of media is electronic games, or video and computer games. Currently there's a lot of discussion about the pros (good points) and cons (bad points) of playing them.

Survey your classmates on their media use. Using the chart below, ask three classmates how many hours a day they spend using the following media. Write the time amounts in the chart.

Time spent each day . . .	Name: _____	Name: _____	Name: _____
·····❯ reading books	_____	_____	_____
·····❯ reading newspapers or magazines	_____	_____	_____
·····❯ watching television	_____	_____	_____
·····❯ listening to the radio	_____	_____	_____
·····❯ listening to an Mp3 player	_____	_____	_____
·····❯ using the Internet	_____	_____	_____
·····❯ playing video or online games with others	_____	_____	_____

Discuss your results with the class.

BUILD *your* vocabulary

 A. **The boldfaced words are from the unit lecture on video games. Listen to each sentence. Then circle the best meaning of the boldfaced word.**

1. The media we use **affects** us in important ways. It impacts not only what we learn, but also how we think about the world.

   a. influences   b. helps

2. Newspapers and other media inform us about current **issues**. They give us information about topics that are important to us.

   a. subjects that people talk about   b. events that are happening

3. Media experts study the **effects** of using different types of media. They try to find out how we are changed by the media we use.

   a. consequences or outcomes   b. opinions

4. Researchers need to gather a lot of **evidence** before making conclusions. They need to gather data and study it carefully to make sure it proves their ideas.

   a. ideas   b. proof

5. Some television shows contain a lot of shooting and fighting. Most media experts agree that young children shouldn't watch these **violent** programs.

   a. using force to hurt someone   b. only for adults

6. Many people are concerned that watching programs with shooting and fighting is bad for children. Will it make them become **aggressive** and try to hurt other children?

   a. not willing to listen to their parent   b. always ready to fight or argue

7. Some psychologists study human **development** from childhood through adulthood.

   a. change over time   b. size

8. One way to study growing children is to observe their **behavior**. Observing children can show us what children do at different ages.

   a. way of writing   b. way of acting

9. Another way to learn about children is to observe their social **interactions**. It's important to see how children act when they play with other children.

   a. communication and behavior with others   b. families

10. Intelligence tests are used to measure a child's **intellectual** abilities. These tests can show a child's ability to think and learn new things.

    a. speaking   b. thinking

11. Some children do poorly on tests because they have short **attention spans**. They are not able to concentrate long enough to answer the questions correctly. As a result, they get poor grades.

    a. number of questions   b. length of time they
       they can answer   can stay focused

12. A **concern** about intelligence tests is that they don't measure all skills. Some worry that certain skills, such as artistic skills, aren't recognized.

    a. worry   b. advice

B. *INTERACT WITH VOCABULARY!* **Work with a partner. Notice the boldfaced words. Reorder the words and write the complete sentence in your notebook. Take turns saying the sentences.**

1. Experts are (the kind of media / **concerned** / that / use / **about** / children).

2. There is (the effects of television / **about** / on / children / **disagreement**).

3. Some say that watching TV has (kids' social development / negative / **on** / **effects**).

4. Many say that violent TV shows cause (**behavior** / children / **in** / aggressive).

5. Some worry that watching TV doesn't teach (others / children / **with** / to **get along**).

6. Studies show (violent / a **connection** / and aggressive behavior / TV shows / **between**).

7. Another concern is that (watching TV / creatively / children / **prevents** / thinking / **from**).

8. Studies show that children are (what they see / **affected** / on TV / **by**).

9. Good school assignments require (students / **between** / **interaction**).

10. Good assignments also allow students to (their own / be creative / and **makes** / stories / **up**).

FOCUS your attention

POINTS OF VIEW

Speakers often explain the opinions, or points of view, on both sides of an issue. They may also provide reasons or evidence to support each side. These phrases introduce the following:

- one side of an issue

> *Critics worry/think . . .*   *Critics say . . .*
>
> *Some argue/think . . .*   *According to . . .*
>
> *Another concern . . .*

- reasons or evidence

> *. . . because . . .*   *In fact, . . .*   *Research shows . . .*
>
> *This is because . . .*   *Studies show . . .*   *One survey found . . .*

- another side of an issue

> *But . . .*   *Others think . . .*
>
> *However, . . .*   *On the other hand, . . .*

TRY IT OUT!

A. Listen to this excerpt from a lecture on video games. What points of view does the speaker mention? Complete the notes as you listen.

B. Compare notes with a partner.

Video Games & Children

Negative Effects	Positive Effects
1. _____ =	1. vision = _____
children don't exercise	2. hand-eye coordination = _____

LISTEN *to the* lecture

BEFORE YOU LISTEN

You are about to listen to this unit's lecture on the effects of video games on the children who play them. What do you think are some negative and positive effects of video games on children?

Video games are bad for children because . . .

1. _____.

2. _____.

Video games are good for children because . . .

1. _____.

2. _____.

LISTEN FOR MAIN IDEAS

A. Close your book. Listen to the lecture and take notes.

B. Use your notes. Complete the outline with the issues discussed in the lecture. Write in the letters of the issues in the order they're discussed in the lecture. Two of the issues are not mentioned.

Survey Results

1. _____

Social Development

2. _____

3. _____

Intellectual Development

4. _____

5. _____

a. ability to concentrate

b. ability to read and write

c. ability to think creatively

d. interaction with other children

e. the number of children who play video games

f. time spent with family

g. violent video games

 A. **Close your book. Listen to the lecture again. Add details to your notes and correct any mistakes.**

B. **Use your notes to decide if the statements below are _T_ (true) or _F_ (false), according to the lecture. Change the false statements to make them true.**

____ 1. A survey found that 77 percent of eight- to seventeen-year-olds in the United States play video games.

____ 2. A study found that 60 percent of game players play games with friends.

____ 3. According to one study, thirteen- and fourteen-year-olds who play violent games are more likely to get into fights.

____ 4. The evidence clearly shows that video games make children aggressive.

____ 5. Some people argue that video games don't teach children to follow directions.

____ 6. Children who play video games have better grades in school than other children.

____ 7. Children learn best when they are entertained.

____ 8. Some games teach children to be creative and to use problem-solving skills.

TALK *about the* topic

A. Listen to the students talk about video games. Read each opinion. Then check (☑) who agrees with it. More than one student may agree.

	Yhinny	Michael	May	Qiang
1. Parents shouldn't let their children play violent games.	☐	☐	☐	☐
2. It's unfair to blame video games for aggressive behavior in kids.	☐	☐	☐	☐

B. Listen to the discussion again. Listen closely for the comments below. Check (☑) the discussion strategy that the student uses.

	Disagreeing	Paraphrasing
1. **Yhinny:** "Wait. I don't think the lecturer said that, exactly."	☐	☐
2. **Yhinny:** "It depends on the game and how much of it you play. Isn't that what she said?"	☐	☐
3. **Michael:** "Well, that's your opinion."	☐	☐
4. **Michael:** "She said the evidence only shows a connection between violent games and aggressive children."	☐	☐

> **Discussion Strategy:** When you **paraphrase**, you restate another person's idea in your own words. Here are some common ways of introducing paraphrased ideas: "What she meant was . . . "; "In other words . . . "; "His point was . . . "; "She basically said . . . ."

C. In small groups, discuss one or more of these topics. Try to use the discussion strategies you have learned.

- Do you think that video games are bad for children? Why or why not?
- Do you play video games? If so, what kinds of games do you like to play? What do you like about them?

R E V I E W *your* **notes**

Work in pairs to complete these notes with information from the lecture.

Effects of video games on children's . . .	The concerns:	What research shows:
social development		
intellectual development		

Now you are ready to take the Unit Test.

TAKE THE UNIT TEST

Tip!

A chart is one way you can organize different points of view on an issue. Each view can go in a row, for easy comparison.

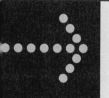# EXTEND *the* topic

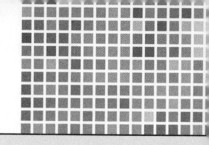

Now you know more about the arguments for and against video game use by children. What's your opinion? The following activities will give you a chance to explore that more.

 A. Listen to this TV show. The host and his guest are debating Internet use by teenagers. Work in pairs to discuss the questions.

1. How does the host, Bob, feel about the Internet? What are his concerns?

2. How does the guest feel about the Internet? What positive effects does she mention?

3. Which opinion about Internet use do you agree with? Why?

4. In what ways can the Internet be dangerous? Give examples.

B. Have a debate about media use. Follow the instructions below.

1. Work in a group. Choose a type of media, such as television, video games, or the Internet.

2. Go online or to the library to research your media choice and make a list of the pros (good points) and cons (bad points) of using it. Include evidence to support the pros and cons.

3. Divide your group into two teams. One side will argue the pros of using the chosen media, and the other side will argue the cons.

4. Perform your debate for the class. First, one team should explain their point of view and provide evidence to support it. Then the other team should disagree with the first team and provide reasons and evidence to support their opinions.

5. While the other groups perform their debates, listen and take notes. What are the pros and cons mentioned by each side? Which team do you think "won" the debate?

UNIT 8

BIOLOGY

Genetically Modified Food

CONNECT *to the* topic

Genetically modified food (also called GM food) is a new type of food. It comes from plants that have been changed in the laboratory. Scientists change the genes inside the plants to make them grow in a different way. A gene is a small part of a cell. It controls the qualities that a parent passes on to its offspring.

Complete the survey by checking (☑) your opinion.

	Strongly disagree	Disagree	Agree	Strongly agree
⋯⋯⟩ We shouldn't change the genes of plants and animals.	____	____	____	____
⋯⋯⟩ I only eat food that is grown without chemicals.	____	____	____	____
⋯⋯⟩ I don't care what I eat, as long as it tastes good.	____	____	____	____
⋯⋯⟩ I want to know where my food comes from.	____	____	____	____
⋯⋯⟩ Scientific research can make food more healthful.	____	____	____	____
⋯⋯⟩ When I shop for food, I care most about low cost.	____	____	____	____
⋯⋯⟩ I would eat genetically modified food.	____	____	____	____

Compare answers in small groups.

BUILD *your* vocabulary

A. The boldfaced words are from the unit lecture on GM food. Listen to the sentences. Guess the meanings of the boldfaced words. Then match the words with their definitions.

____ 1. *E. coli* **bacteria** are very dangerous. If food has these bacteria on it, people can become very sick or die.

____ 2. Doctors say we should **consume** eight glasses of water each day, including the water in the food we eat and in the things we drink.

____ 3. Farmers grow **crops** such as wheat and corn.

    a. plants that are grown for food
    b. very small living things that sometimes cause disease
    c. to eat or drink

____ 4. Most strawberry plants grow in warm places. However, scientists want to **modify** strawberry plants so they can live in cold weather.

____ 5. The weather this year was **normal**. We had the usual amount of rain and snow.

____ 6. I used a **pesticide** to kill the ants in my kitchen.

    a. usual and expected
    b. to make small changes to something
    c. a poisonous chemical used to kill insects

____ 7. When the apples are ready to eat, the farmer **picks** them from the tree.

____ 8. The corn grown in the United States is used **primarily** for feeding animals. Most corn is fed to cows, pigs, and chickens, not people.

____ 9. We **purchase** most of our vegetables from local farmers, not a supermarket.

    a. to pull a fruit or vegetable from a plant
    b. to buy
    c. mainly

___ 10. I put the carrots in the refrigerator so they **retain** their freshness. If I don't, they get soft and don't taste good.

___ 11. Oceans are one **source** of fish. Fish farms, lakes, and rivers are others.

___ 12. My mother gave us **vitamins** every day. We took vitamin A for healthy eyes and vitamin D for strong bones.

    a. a place where you get something
    b. to keep or hold on to
    c. a part of food that helps with good health

B. INTERACT WITH VOCABULARY! Work with a partner. Notice the boldfaced words. Circle the best word to complete each sentence. Take turns saying the sentences.

1. (Genetically / Gene) **modified food** is made in the laboratory.

2. Scientists (modify / modifying) **genes** to make plants grow differently.

3. Scientists want to (solve / solved) **problems**.

4. *E. coli* are (common / commonly) **bacteria**.

5. **Just** (picked / picking) **fruit** is delicious.

6. Corn (stays / staying) **fresh** in the refrigerator.

7. Some people are against the (use / used) **of pesticides** to kill insects.

8. Our corn crop was (consumed / consumer) **by insects**.

9. Farmers (grow / grown) **crops** to sell.

10. Vegetables are a good (source / sources) **of vitamins**.

11. I didn't feel like shopping; I quickly (made / make) **a purchase** and then left the store.

12. Tomatoes don't **retain their** (flavor / flavored) after you pick them.

FOCUS *your* attention

KEY TERMS

Speakers often introduce important new terms in a lecture. They may explain how the term is pronounced or spelled. Listen for new terms so that you can write them down in your notes.

Speakers often signal an important term by doing the following:

- emphasizing the term by saying it louder or longer
- repeating the term
- pausing before and/or after the term
- spelling the term
- making a hand gesture that goes with the term
- writing the term on the board

TRY IT OUT!

A. **Listen to this excerpt from a lecture on biology. What key terms does the speaker introduce? Complete the notes as you listen.**

B. **Compare notes with a partner.**

Biology

Today: _____

- change genes inside living thing
- plant/animal grows differently

Also called: _____

LISTEN *to the* **lecture**

BEFORE YOU LISTEN

You are about to listen to this unit's lecture on genetically modified food. Based on what you've heard about GM food, what do you think the speaker's opinion will be? Circle your answer.

a. GM food is dangerous.

b. GM food can help people live better lives.

c. GM food is difficult to create.

LISTEN FOR MAIN IDEAS

A. **Close your book. Listen to the lecture and take notes.**

B. **Use your notes. Based on the information in the lecture, match the type of food with the reason it was developed. One reason is not mentioned in the lecture.**

Food

_____ 1. FlavrSavr Tomato was developed to . . .

_____ 2. Bt Corn was developed to . . .

_____ 3. Golden Rice was developed to . . .

Reason

a. grow better.   c. solve a health problem.
b. cost less.   d. stay fresh longer.

LISTEN FOR DETAILS

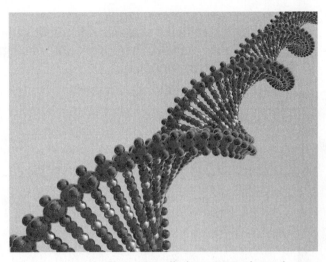

Genes are part of what is called our DNA, shown here.
DNA is inside every cell of all living things.

 A. **Close your book. Listen to the lecture again. Add details to your notes and correct any mistakes.**

B. **Use your notes. Mark the statements *T* (true) or *F* (false).**

1. The FlavrSavr Tomato . . .

____ has a gene that stops the tomato from changing color.

____ was the first genetically modified food sold in U.S. supermarkets.

____ was popular because shoppers thought it was healthier.

____ is sold in supermarkets today.

2. Bt Corn . . .

____ is used instead of pesticides.

____ kills insects but doesn't hurt people or animals.

____ has a gene that comes from another plant.

____ is used by farmers all over the world.

3. Golden Rice . . .

____ helps people who eat too much fat.

____ could stop death and blindness in millions of children.

____ has a vitamin A gene from a flower.

____ is being studied to make it less expensive.

TALK *about the* topic

A. Listen to the students talk about genetically modified food. Read each opinion. Then check (☑) who agrees with it. More than one student may agree.

	May	Qiang	Yhinny	Michael
1. I don't trust GM food.	☐	☐	☐	☐
2. I support GM food.	☐	☐	☐	☐
3. I think that big business wants to make money from GM food.	☐	☐	☐	☐

May

Qiang

Yhinny

Michael

B. Listen to the discussion again. Listen closely for the comments below. Check (☑) the discussion strategy that the student uses.

	Offering a fact or example	Keeping the discussion on topic	Trying to reach a consensus
1. **Michael:** "There are a lot of governments that won't even let these foods come into their countries."	☐	☐	☐
2. **Qiang:** "I mean, look at Bt Corn—it takes away the need for pesticides."	☐	☐	☐
3. **Michael:** "OK. Maybe we should just 'agree to disagree' on this one?"	☐	☐	☐
4. **May:** "Let's get back to our notes."	☐	☐	☐

> **Discussion Strategy:** Getting a group to **reach a consensus**, or agree, can be challenging. One approach is to use questions to identify areas of agreement ("So, when is everyone free to meet again?"). You can then make suggestions based on how people answered your question ("Sounds like Sunday is open for everyone—does that work?").

C. In small groups, discuss one or more of these topics. Try to use the discussion strategies you have learned.

- Do you think genetically modified food is safe to eat? Why or why not?
- Should governments allow genetically modified food to be grown? Why or why not?
- What other health or environmental problems could be solved by creating new genetically modified crops? Give an example.

REVIEW *your* notes

Work in pairs. Using your notes, discuss and complete the notes below with information from the lecture.

Genetic modification def.:

	FlavrSavr Tomato	Bt Corn	Golden Rice
Why developed?			
How modified?			
What modification does:			
# of people using today:			
Other:			

Now you are ready to take the Unit Test.

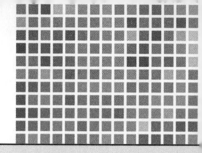

EXTEND *the* topic

You've learned about different kinds of genetically modified food. Now use that knowledge in the following activities, including interviewing others about GM foods.

A. Listen to this public radio report on places that require labels for GM food. Then check (☑) the places that require labels.

___ Japan   ___ United States
___ European Union   ___ Argentina

Does your country require labels for GM foods? Do you think labels should be required? Explain your opinion.

B. Take a survey on food and health. Work in a group. Look at the survey together. Then prepare a definition of *genetically modified food* in case you need to explain the term.

Working alone, use the chart below to interview four people outside of class about GM food.

Part 1 Would you eat genetically modified food? Why or why not? _____		Yes	No	Maybe

Part 2 How often do you eat . . .	Never	A few times/ month	A few times/ week	Every day
a. in restaurants?	1	2	3	4
b. fast food?	1	2	3	4
c. sweets, such as candy or cake?	1	2	3	4
d. fried food?	1	2	3	4
e. meat?	1	2	3	4
f. food made with artificial chemicals, such as flavors or colors?	1	2	3	4
Total _____ = ___ + ___ + ___ + ___				

Part 2 How often do you eat . . .	Never	A few times/ month	A few times/ week	Every day
g. home-cooked food?	1	2	3	4
h. natural or organic food?	1	2	3	4
i. fresh fruit or vegetables?	1	2	3	4
j. chicken or fish?	1	2	3	4
k. beans, soybeans, or tofu?	1	2	3	4
Total _____	= ___	+ ___	+ ___	+ ___

Record the answers here.

	Person 1	Person 2	Person 3	Person 4
Would eat GM food: **Yes, No, or Maybe**				
Score for a–f:				
Score for g–k:				

C. Meet in small groups. Look at the meaning of each person's score for Part 2.

Score/Results	Eats very healthy food	Eats somewhat healthy food	Eats somewhat unhealthy food	Eats very unhealthy food
a–f	6–8	9–14	15–20	21–24
g–k	18–20	13–17	8–12	5–7

Then look at the person's answers for Part 1. What conclusions can you make? What seems to be the connection between what people eat and how they feel about GM food? Share your answers from the survey and discuss.

UNIT 9

The Search for Extraterrestrial Intelligence

CONNECT *to the* topic

Astronomy is the scientific study of the stars and planets in the universe. Some astronomers think about this question: Is there extraterrestrial life (life on other planets)? Many other people also find this idea fascinating. Books, television shows, and movies show images of aliens from other planets. Some people believe that aliens have come to Earth. What do you think?

Read each statement. Check (☑) your opinion.

	Agree	Disagree
⋯⟩ There is extraterrestrial life somewhere in the universe.	____	____
⋯⟩ There are aliens who are intelligent like human beings.	____	____
⋯⟩ Aliens want to communicate with us.	____	____
⋯⟩ Aliens have visited Earth.	____	____
⋯⟩ Aliens want to hurt us.	____	____
⋯⟩ We should try to communicate with aliens.	____	____

Discuss your answers in a small group. Give reasons for your opinions.

BUILD *your* vocabulary

A. The boldfaced words are from the unit lecture on the SETI Project. Listen to the sentences. Then match the words with their definitions.

____ 1. I **assume** that people will travel to Mars one day. We've already been to the moon, and I think Mars is next.

____ 2. There are more than six and a half **billion** people alive on Earth today, and that number will continue to grow.

____ 3. In Morse code, letters are made with a **sequence** of long and short beeps. For example, the letter *A* is a short then long beep.

    a. the number 1 followed by nine zeros
    b. a series of events that happen in order
    c. to think something is true based on available information

____ 4. Earth's galaxy is the Milky Way **galaxy**. The Milky Way galaxy contains billions of stars and planets, including our solar system.

____ 5. A few people believe that the rocket was **intentionally** destroyed. Most people believe it was an accident.

____ 6. The Milky Way galaxy is about 100,000 **light years** wide. It would take 100,000 years for light to travel from one side of the galaxy to the other.

    a. the distance that light travels in one year
    b. on purpose; not by mistake
    c. a large group of stars

____ 7. The planet Earth is the third planet from the sun. It is **located** between Venus and Mars.

____ 8. Scientists are taking pictures of the galaxy. This **project** will take many years.

____ 9. We can't count the stars in the universe, but scientists can **estimate** the number.

    a. a carefully planned piece of work
    b. to guess about something
    c. set in a particular place

_____ 10. Astronomers are looking for a **signal** from space. They're searching for any signs of life.

_____ 11. Some businesses are developing **spaceships** to take tourists into space.

_____ 12. New **technology**, such as strong telescopes, has helped us learn more about the universe.

    a. *machines made with the knowledge of modern science and computers*
    b. *a vehicle that carries people through space*
    c. *a sound or action you make to give someone information*

B. **INTERACT WITH VOCABULARY!** Work with a partner. Student A: Read aloud sentences 1–5 in Column 1. Student B: Listen and complete the sentences in Column 2. Notice the boldfaced words. Switch roles for 6–10.

Column 1	**Column 2**
1. We are **listening for** a signal.	1. We are **listening** _____ a signal.
2. I think aliens will **communicate with** us.	2. I think aliens will **communicate** _____ us.
3. Is there anyone else **in the universe**?	3. Is there anyone else _____ **the universe**?
4. There's a huge **number of** stars in our galaxy.	4. There's a huge **number** _____ stars in our galaxy.
5. I'd like to **travel by** spaceship.	5. I'd like to **travel** _____ spaceship.
6. Scientists are **searching for** extraterrestrial life.	6. Scientists are **searching** _____ extraterrestrial life.
7. Radio signals **travel at** the speed of light.	7. Radio signals **travel** _____ the speed of light.
8. Scientists **all over the world** are studying space.	8. Scientists **all** _____ **the world** are studying space.
9. We should protect life **on Earth**.	9. We should protect life _____ **Earth**.
10. Earth has the right **conditions for life**.	10. Earth has the right **conditions** _____ **life**.

FOCUS *your* attention

DEGREES OF CERTAINTY

Speakers often express how certain they are about something. They may describe information that they are certain is true, such as facts. They may also discuss theories that they think are probably true or possibilities that may or may not be true. It is important to listen for the differences among these three types of ideas.

Fact (certain):

> *Mars is the fourth planet from the sun.*
> *In 1965, the spaceship Mariner 4 took the first pictures of Mars.*

Theory (probable, but not proven):

> *It's very probable that . . .*   *It makes sense that . . .*
> *It's likely that . . .*   *We assume that . . .*

Possibility (less certain):

> *Maybe . . .*   *It's possible that . . .*
> *There may/could be . . .*   *We think that . . .*

TRY IT OUT!

A. **Listen to this excerpt from a lecture about Mars. Listen closely for the statements below. Complete the notes. Then check (☑) whether the idea is a fact or theory/possibility.**

B. **Compare notes with a partner.**

NASA scientists:		Fact	Theory/Possibility
there could be _____ on the planet Mars			
spaceship took pictures _____			
probable: some kind of _____ on Mars			
assume: no life there now			

LISTEN *to the* lecture

Radio telescopes

BEFORE YOU LISTEN

You are about to listen to this unit's lecture on the SETI Project. *SETI* stands for the Search for Extraterrestrial Intelligence.

a. How do you think scientists are searching for alien life?

_____

b. What have they found?

_____

LISTEN FOR MAIN IDEAS

A. **Close your book. Listen to the lecture and take notes.**

B. **Use your notes. Circle *a*, *b*, or *c*, based on the lecture.**

1. Many scientists _____ other intelligent beings in the universe.

    a. have found signs of

    b. assume there are

    c. do not think there are

2. There are many planets in the universe that _____.

    a. are probably like Earth and could have intelligent life

    b. we can reach by rocket

    c. are sending signals to us

3. The SETI Project searches for _____.

    a. alien spaceships traveling through space

    b. radio signals from other planets

    c. other planets like Earth

4. The speaker feels that the SETI search _____.

    a. is dangerous

    b. is a good idea

    c. won't be successful

LISTEN FOR DETAILS

A. **Close your book. Listen to the lecture again. Add details to your notes and correct any mistakes.**

B. **Use your notes. Complete the sentences based on the lecture.**

1. _____ create the right conditions for life on Earth.

    a. Sunlight and water   b. Air and oceans

2. There are about _____ stars in the Milky Way.

    a. 100 billion   b. 200 billion

3. There are about _____ other galaxies in the universe.

    a. 100 billion   b. 200 billion

4. It would take a rocket _____ years to reach Alpha Centauri.

    a. 4.2   b. 60,000

5. SETI uses large radio telescopes located _____.

    a. around the world   b. in North America

6. The technology to make radio signals is not very _____.

    a. complicated   b. expensive

7. It would take a radio signal _____ years to travel from Alpha Centauri to Earth.

    a. four   b. sixty

8. SETI is searching for a signal that is strong and _____.

    a. contains language   b. has a sequence

TALK *about the* topic

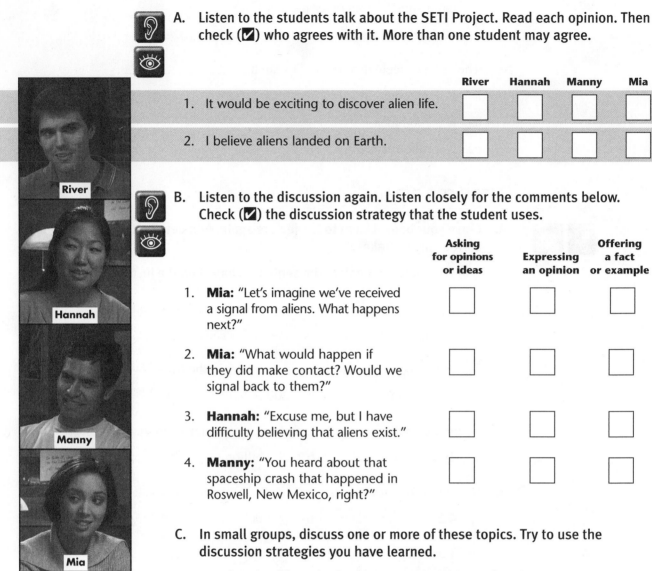

A. Listen to the students talk about the SETI Project. Read each opinion. Then check (☑) who agrees with it. More than one student may agree.

	River	Hannah	Manny	Mia
1. It would be exciting to discover alien life.	☐	☐	☐	☐
2. I believe aliens landed on Earth.	☐	☐	☐	☐

B. Listen to the discussion again. Listen closely for the comments below. Check (☑) the discussion strategy that the student uses.

	Asking for opinions or ideas	Expressing an opinion	Offering a fact or example
1. **Mia:** "Let's imagine we've received a signal from aliens. What happens next?"	☐	☐	☐
2. **Mia:** "What would happen if they did make contact? Would we signal back to them?"	☐	☐	☐
3. **Hannah:** "Excuse me, but I have difficulty believing that aliens exist."	☐	☐	☐
4. **Manny:** "You heard about that spaceship crash that happened in Roswell, New Mexico, right?"	☐	☐	☐

C. In small groups, discuss one or more of these topics. Try to use the discussion strategies you have learned.

- What should we do if we receive a signal from aliens?
- Would communicating with aliens make the world better or worse? How?
- Do you think that space research, including the SETI Project, is useful, or do you think we should spend our time and money on projects here on Earth?

R E V I E W *your* notes

According to the lecture, SETI scientists make some assumptions in their search for extraterrestrial intelligence. Use your notes to complete the chart below with the facts or theories/possibilities that support those assumptions.

Assumptions	Facts	Theories/Possibilities
There are other planets in the universe that could support life.		
Aliens will not travel to Earth by spaceship.		
Aliens will communicate by sending radio signals.		

Now you are ready to take the Unit Test.

Tip!

Remember: Facts are true, but theories and possibilities may not be. Be sure you understand which is which in your notes.

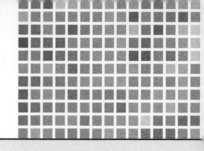

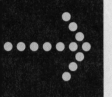 # E X T E N D *the* topic

You've studied how scientists are searching for signals from other planets. Now learn about other space projects.

A. **Listen to a talk show host's monologue about communicating with extraterrestrials. Then complete these statements.**

1. The United States sent a Beatles song into space to celebrate

   _____ years of U.S. space missions.

2. They sent it toward Polaris, the North Star, which is

   _____ light years away.

3. Radio, TV, and satellite signals have been going into space for the past

   _____ years.

Discuss these questions with your classmates.

If you could send a song into space to represent Earth, what song would you send? Why?

B. **Read about information that we have sent into outer space.**

In 1977, two *Voyager* spaceships were sent into space to explore our galaxy and beyond. Each *Voyager* spaceship carries a golden record with information about life on Earth. The record contains 115 pictures from around the world. It also has recordings of a variety of sounds: sounds from nature, music from different cultures, and greetings in fifty-five languages.

Today, the two *Voyager* spaceships are both near the edge of our solar system. They are the only human-made objects to travel so far into space. Scientists hope that if any extraterrestrials find either one of the golden records, they will use the information to learn about Earth.

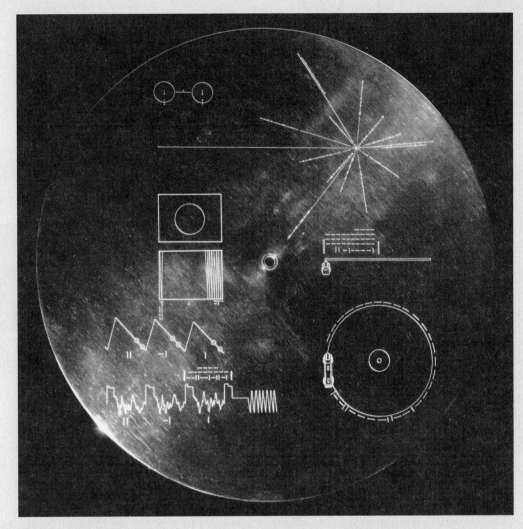

One of the golden records sent into space, containing photos and sounds of Earth

C. Work in a small group. Follow the instructions below.

1. Think about what parts of life on Earth you want to show the aliens: human life, nature, technology, art, and so on. Do you want to show only positive things, or both positive and negative things?

2. Decide on ten things to represent the different parts of life on Earth. They can be objects, recordings, pictures, computer files, or other things. However, remember that aliens might not have the same technology that we do. Discuss your reasons for choosing each thing.

3. Present your list to the class. Explain the reasons for your choices.

UNIT 10

Shackleton

Clockwise from left: Mt. Everest explorers Sir Edmund Hillary and Tenzing Norgay, 1953; Sir Ernest Shackleton's ship the *Endurance* stuck in the ice in Antarctica, 1915; primatologist Jane Goodall studying chimps in Tanzania, 2006

CONNECT *to the* **topic**

In the early 1900s, explorers wanted to learn all they possibly could about the world. In 1914, explorer Sir Ernest Shackleton began planning a journey to Antarctica. He put an ad in a London paper. He received 5,000 applications.

Work in a small group. Imagine that you have to pick people to go on Shackleton's trip to Antarctica. Choose your top five qualities from the list below or add your own.

····> bravery

····> physical strength

····> intelligence

····> education

····> good communication skills

····> ability to work well with others

····> experience on a ship

····> knowledge of Antarctica

> **Men Wanted**
>
> For dangerous journey. Low pay, freezing cold, long months of complete darkness, constant danger, safe return doubtful. Honor and recognition in case of success.
>
> *Sir Ernest Shackleton*

Share your choices with the class. Explain your reasoning.

BUILD your vocabulary

 A. **The boldfaced words are from the unit lecture on Sir Ernest Shackleton. Listen to the sentences. Then circle the best meaning of the boldfaced word.**

1. In 1913, explorer Vihjalmur Stefansson led a trip on the ship the *Karluck* to the North Pole. He had a **crew** of thirteen sailors, ten scientists, and eight other people.

   a. people who work on a ship   b. people who travel by ship

2. The *Karluck* **sailed** north toward the Arctic Circle.

   a. traveled over land   b. traveled over water while pushed by wind

3. Soon, the ship became **stuck** in the ice and didn't move for three weeks. The ice floated slowly north, taking the ship with it.

   a. unable to stop   b. unable to move

4. Stefansson did not care about his crew or treat them with **respect**. Instead of staying with them, he took five men and left the ship. He never returned to get the crew.

   a. concern and thoughtfulness   b. anger and rudeness

5. However, ship's officer Bob Bartlett took care of the crew even though it wasn't his job. This showed **leadership**.

   a. being a leader   b. following a leader

6. Bartlett **ordered** the crew off the ship and onto the ice. Everyone did what he said.

   a. told someone to do something   b. asked someone to do something

7. The ship was finally **crushed** by the ice, breaking it into many pieces.

   a. made a big hole in something   b. pressed so hard that something breaks

8. The ship **sank** under the water.

   a. turned on one side   b. went below the water

9. The crew **survived** on the ice by catching birds and other animals to eat.

   a. continued to live   b. continued to travel

10. Bartlett tried to keep the crew's **morale** up, but they were depressed and fearful.

   a. belief about right and wrong   b. level of positive feelings

11. With the goal of getting help, Bartlett took a small **team** of men and left.

a. a group of people who dislike each other

b. a group of people who work together

12. Meanwhile, another ship **rescued** the crew in September 1914.

a. saved

b. left

13. During the eight months they lived on the ice, eleven people died. However, the crew **credited** Bartlett with trying to save them.

a. believed he made a mistake

b. believed he did something good

14. Today, Bartlett is remembered as a hero for being **loyal** to the crew, while Stefansson is remembered for leaving his men to die on the ice.

a. always supporting other people

b. thinking only of oneself

B. **INTERACT WITH VOCABULARY!** Work in pairs. Student A: Read aloud sentence starters 1–7 from Column 1. Student B: Listen and complete each sentence with a phrase from Column 2. Notice the boldfaced words. Switch roles for 8–14.

Column 1	**Column 2**
1. Stefansson began an **exploration**	a. **in** the ice.
2. Stefansson didn't **treat** the crew	b. **the order** to leave the boat.
3. Stefansson didn't **interact** well	c. **signs of** poor leadership.
4. The ship became **stuck**	d. **of** the North Pole.
5. By leaving the ship, Stefansson **showed**	e. **under** the water.
6. Bartlett **gave**	f. **with respect**.
7. The ice crushed the ship, and it **sank**	g. **with** his men.

8. Bartlett tried to **keep**	h. **together** as a team.
9. The men **worked**	i. **by a boat**.
10. The men **survived**	j. **up** the crew's morale.
11. The crew was **loyal**	k. **to** Bartlett.
12. The men were **rescued**	l. **as a hero** for rescuing the men.
13. Bartlett was **credited**	m. **by** staying positive.
14. Bartlett is **remembered**	n. **with** saving the crew.

FOCUS *your* attention

CHRONOLOGICAL ORDER (TIME)

When speakers discuss events in history, they often describe the events in chronological (time) order. Listen for the dates and periods of time. In speech, dates are usually expressed with ordinal numbers such as *first, tenth,* and *thirtieth.* When you take notes, abbreviate the dates by writing them as numbers. Notice the following abbreviations: ~ = about; < = less than; > = more than. On the left is what you hear. On the right is how it's written.

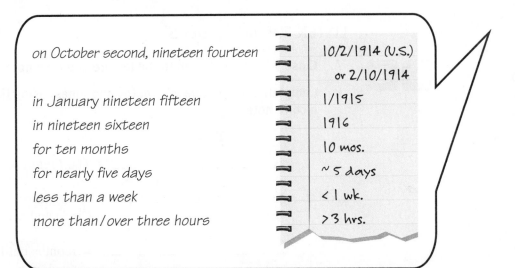

on October second, nineteen fourteen	10/2/1914 (U.S.) or 2/10/1914
in January nineteen fifteen	1/1915
in nineteen sixteen	1916
for ten months	10 mos.
for nearly five days	~ 5 days
less than a week	< 1 wk.
more than/over three hours	> 3 hrs.

TRY IT OUT!

A. **Listen to this excerpt from a history lecture. Complete the notes below as you listen.**

B. **Compare notes with a partner.**

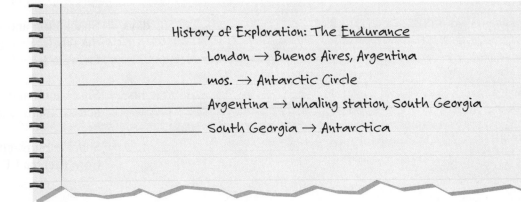

History of Exploration: The <u>Endurance</u>

_____ London → Buenos Aires, Argentina

_____ mos. → Antarctic Circle

_____ Argentina → whaling station, South Georgia

_____ South Georgia → Antarctica

LISTEN *to the* lecture

BEFORE YOU LISTEN

You are about to listen to this unit's lecture on Shackleton and his ship, the *Endurance*. Look at the map of the journey of the *Endurance* on page 97. Think about these questions.

1. How long do you think the trip lasted?

2. Why do you think people remember the trip today?

LISTEN FOR MAIN IDEAS

A. Close your book. Listen to the lecture and take notes.

B. Complete the timeline with dates and times, using the map and your lecture notes.

Date/Time

1. _____ The *Endurance* left England.

Ⓐ 2. _____ The *Endurance* entered the Antarctic Circle and became stuck in the ice.

3. _____ = months until spring begins.

Ⓑ 4. _____ = Shackleton ordered the crew off the ship.

5. _____ = The *Endurance* sank.

6. _____ = The ice began to melt.

Ⓒ 7. _____ = The crew traveled in small boats to Elephant Island.

Ⓓ 8. _____ days = Shackleton and five men sailed to the whaling station on South Georgia Island.

9. _____ hrs. = Shackleton and his men walked across South Georgia Island.

10. _____ = Shackleton rescued all of his men from Elephant Island.

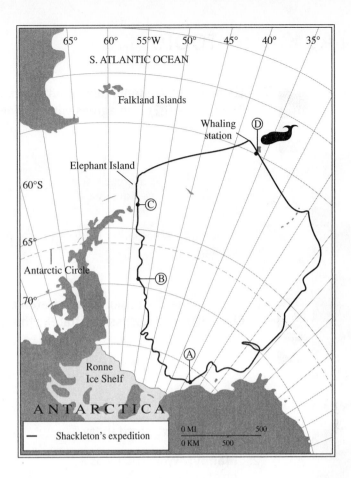

LISTEN FOR DETAILS

A. Close your book. Listen to the lecture again. Add details to your notes and correct any mistakes.

B. Use your notes. Mark the statements *T* (true) or *F* (false), based on the lecture.

_____ 1. Shackleton's goal was to sail around Antarctica.

_____ 2. The *Endurance*'s crew included ship's officers, sailors, and scientists.

_____ 3. Shackleton had crew members work together to get work done quickly.

_____ 4. In October 1915, the crew moved onto the ice because the ship was full.

_____ 5. When the crew reached Elephant Island, it was the first time in more than a year that they had stood on land.

_____ 6. Shackleton and five men traveled eighty miles by boat to South Georgia.

_____ 7. The South Georgia station manager thought Shackleton and his crew were dead.

_____ 8. Shackleton rescued his crew on Elephant Island right away.

TALK *about the* topic

A. Listen to the students talk about Shackleton's journey. Read each opinion. Then check (☑) who agrees with it. More than one student may agree.

	Mia	Manny	Hannah	River
1. Shackleton was a great leader because he treated everyone equally.	☐	☐	☐	☐
2. Shackleton was a great leader because he made important decisions.	☐	☐	☐	☐

B. Listen to the discussion again. Listen closely for the comments below. Check (☑) the discussion strategy that the student uses.

	Asking for opinions or ideas	Expressing an opinion	Keeping the discussion on topic
1. **River:** "Guys, I think we're supposed to be talking about the lecture we heard today."	☐	☐	☐
2. **Manny:** "Wow! That was a great story!"	☐	☐	☐
3. **Hannah:** "Yeah, so, I'm curious about everyone's thoughts . . . "	☐	☐	☐
4. **Manny:** "People need great leaders, or they just panic or give up."	☐	☐	☐

Photographs labeled: Mia, Manny, Hannah, River

> **Discussion Strategy:** In study groups or other organized conversations, **keeping the discussion on topic** is sometimes difficult. "Tangents" (related topics) can be interesting, but it's important to remind others to focus on the main topic of your discussion. You can remind others by using expressions such as "I'd like to get back to . . . "; "We're getting a little off track . . . "; and the very informal "Anyway!"

C. In small groups, discuss one or more of these quotations. What does it mean? Would Shackleton and his crew agree with it? Try to use the discussion strategies you have learned.

- "Exploration is the essence of the human spirit."—Frank Borman, astronaut
- "To lead people, walk beside them."—Lao-Tzu, Chinese philosopher
- "The first task of a leader is to keep hope alive."—Joe Batten, author
- "To be a leader, a person must have followers. And to have followers, a person must have their trust."—Dwight D. Eisenhower, U.S. president

REVIEW *your* notes

Work with a partner. Complete the timeline with dates and important events in the story of Shackleton and the *Endurance*. Use your notes from the lecture.

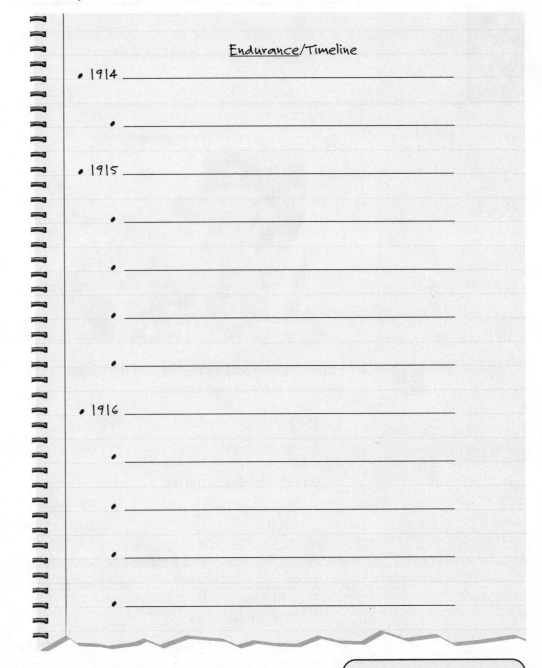

Endurance/Timeline

- 1914 _____
- _____
- 1915 _____
- _____
- _____
- _____
- 1916 _____
- _____
- _____
- _____
- _____

Now you are ready to take the Unit Test.

> **Tip!**
>
> A timeline can help you see the chronological order of events. It can also help you see "the big picture," or how individual events look all together.

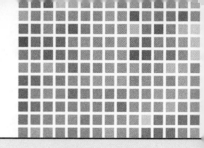

E X T E N D *the* topic

You've learned about Shackleton's exploration of Antarctica in the early 1900s. Now learn about other explorers and adventurers.

The crewmembers of *Apollo 13* departed for the moon April 11, 1970.

 A. **Listen to this report on the flight of the *Apollo 13* space mission. Then circle the letter of the correct answer.**

1. The goal of the *Apollo 13* flight was to _____.

   a. fly around the moon   b. land on the moon

2. On the third day of the flight, _____.

   a. there was an explosion   b. the ship's computers
      on the ship   stopped working

3. The crew had problems because the spaceship _____.

   a. stopped moving   b. lost air, power, and water

4. The flight ended when _____.

   a. the crew died in space   b. the spaceship landed safely
                                          in the ocean

Discuss these questions in a small group.

1. What are the similarities between the trip of the *Endurance* to Antarctica and the trip of *Apollo 13* into space?

2. What are the differences?

B. Research an explorer or adventurer. Choose one of the people below or find someone else you're interested in.

····} Yuri Gagarin, first human in space

····} Neil Armstrong and Edwin "Buzz" Adrin Jr., first humans on the moon

····} Jacques Cousteau, ocean explorer

····} Jane Goodall, researcher of chimpanzees in the African jungle

····} Christopher Columbus, explorer of the "new world"

····} Sir Edmund Hillary and Tenzing Norgay, first to climb Mount Everest

····} Amelia Earhart, first woman to fly alone across the Atlantic Ocean

····} Junko Tabei, first woman to climb Mount Everest

Complete the chart below with information about the person. Then make a presentation to the class.

Name	
Nationality	
Exploration/ Adventure & date	
Why remembered as history	

PHILOSOPHY
Ethics

CONNECT *to the* topic

Ethics are rules that help people decide what is right and wrong. We learn ethics from our family, religion, and culture. Philosophers study ethics and try to describe how people make ethical decisions.

Work in a small group. Read each situation. What would be the ethical thing to do in each situation? Explain your choices.

┈┈▹ Rita finds an envelope on the ground. Inside the envelope is $1,000 in cash. There is a name and address on the envelope.

┈┈▹ A doctor tells Jim that he has a serious disease. Jim says he feels fine, but the doctor explains that the disease could spread easily to other people. The doctor tells Jim not to travel or spend time in crowded places. However, Jim already has a vacation to Europe planned.

BUILD *your* vocabulary

A. The boldfaced words are from the unit lecture on ethics. Listen to each sentence. Then match the words with their definitions.

____ 1. It's important to think about how your **actions** affect other people. When you do something, consider the overall effect: Will it help or hurt them?

____ 2. People can't smoke cigarettes in our office building, so the company **allows** employees to go outside to smoke.

____ 3. My city **banned** cell phone use while driving. Drivers have to stop their cars to make cell phone calls.

      a. to stop or disallow
      b. to let someone do something
      c. things you do

____ 4. Government leaders should make decisions that are good for the whole **community**, not just some of the people.

____ 5. We need to make our own **individual** decisions, not copy what everyone else does. For example, some people refuse to pay taxes.

____ 6. A few people are against the new no-smoking law, but the **majority** support it.

      a. as a single person, separate from the society one lives in
      b. most of the people in a group
      c. a group of people who live in the same area

____ 7. It's important to have **freedom** to choose your religion. It's unethical for some.

____ 8. Governments should spend money where it will do the **greatest good** and help the most people.

____ 9. I believe it is wrong to hurt or kill animals. Because of this **principle**, I don't eat meat.

      a. the ability to do what you want, without being controlled by others
      b. the most positive effect
      c. a belief about what is right or wrong that affects how you behave

_____ 10. The government gives the people the **right** of free speech. That means that people are free to say what they want, and the government can't stop them.

_____ 11. We have to pay a **tax** on everything we buy. The government uses that extra money to pay for schools and roads.

_____ 12. I wanted to buy cigarettes, but I made the more **utilitarian** choice and spent my last $20 on groceries.

     a. *money you must pay to the government for use in public services*
     b. *something that you can ethically or legally do*
     c. *useful*

B. *INTERACT WITH VOCABULARY!* **Work with a partner. Notice the boldfaced words. Reorder the words and write the complete sentence in your notebook. Take turns saying the sentences.**

1. I believe in (**freedom** / make / **to** / choices / **the**).

2. Every day individuals (**about** / **choices** / **make** / must) what is best.

3. We don't always know (**the effects** / our actions / **of** / on) other people.

4. Ethical principles (help / **decisions** / **make** / us / good).

5. Sometimes utilitarian decisions serve (**in** / only / the greater good / **principle**).

6. Some people want (to / free / **on** / **put** / speech / **ban** / **a**).

7. However, most people believe in (**the** / free / **right** / **to** / speech).

8. The (people / **of** / community / **majority** / in / my) agree with me.

9. Many people (**issue** / **have** / **with** / **an**) smoking in public places.

10. Every individual (**to** / **be** / should / **allowed** / enjoy) freedom of expression.

FOCUS *your* attention

EXAMPLES

Speakers use examples to explain their ideas. Here are some phrases that signal examples:

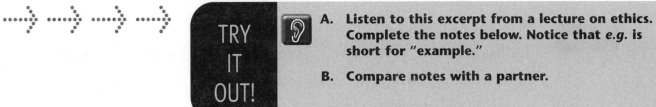

> For instance . . .
> For example . . .
> Let's take _____ as an example . . .
> Let's look at an example . . .
> Let's say that . . .
> Through this example, we can see . . .

TRY IT OUT!

A. **Listen to this excerpt from a lecture on ethics. Complete the notes below. Notice that *e.g.* is short for "example."**

B. **Compare notes with a partner.**

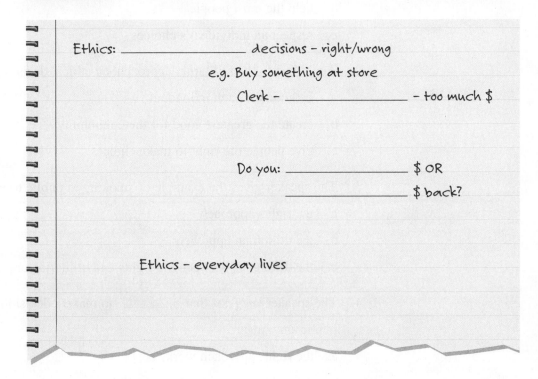

Ethics: _____ decisions – right/wrong

         e.g. Buy something at store

             Clerk – _____ – too much $

             Do you: _____ $ OR

                   _____ $ back?

Ethics – everyday lives

LISTEN *to the* **lecture**

BEFORE YOU LISTEN

You're about to listen to this unit's lecture on ethical decision making. The speaker will discuss two approaches: the rights approach and the utilitarian approach. Based on the meanings of the words *rights* and *utilitarian*, how do you think these two terms will be defined?

The rights approach: An ethical decision is an action that is _____

_____.

The utilitarian approach: An ethical decision is an action that is _____

_____.

LISTEN FOR MAIN IDEAS

A. **Close your book. Listen to the lecture and take notes.**

B. **Use your notes. Circle the best answer, based on the lecture.**

1. According to the rights approach, an ethical decision must _____.

   a. be agreed to by each individual

   b. help the most people

   c. respect an individual's choices

2. According to the utilitarian approach, an ethical decision must _____.

   a. be good for each individual

   b. create the greatest good for the community

   c. give people the right to make choices

3. The speaker gives the example of smoking in public to illustrate _____.

   a. the rights approach

   b. the utilitarian approach

   c. the difference between the rights and utilitarian approaches

4. The speaker suggests that _____ to make a decision about public smoking.

   a. the rights approach works best

   b. the utilitarian approach works best

   c. the rights and utilitarian approaches work equally well

LISTEN FOR DETAILS

A. Close your book. Listen to the lecture again. Add details to your notes and correct any mistakes.

B. Use your notes. Check (☑) the approach that the sentence is describing, based on the lecture.

	Individual rights	Utilitarianism
1. This idea is from the philosophy of Immanuel Kant.	✓	
2. This idea was made popular by John Stuart Mill.		✓
3. People must respect an individual's freedom to speak.		
4. Individuals must pay taxes to help the community.		
5. What action will mean the greatest good?		
6. How does this affect a person's freedom to choose?		
7. Smokers should be free to smoke because everyone is free to make his or her own decisions about health.		
8. Nonsmokers should be free to breathe clean air because smoking is bad for public health.		
9. Smoking should be allowed in order to please smokers.		
10. Smoking creates a lot of health problems for the community, so it should be banned.		
11. Smoking should be banned if we want to save money in our health care system.		

TALK *about the* topic

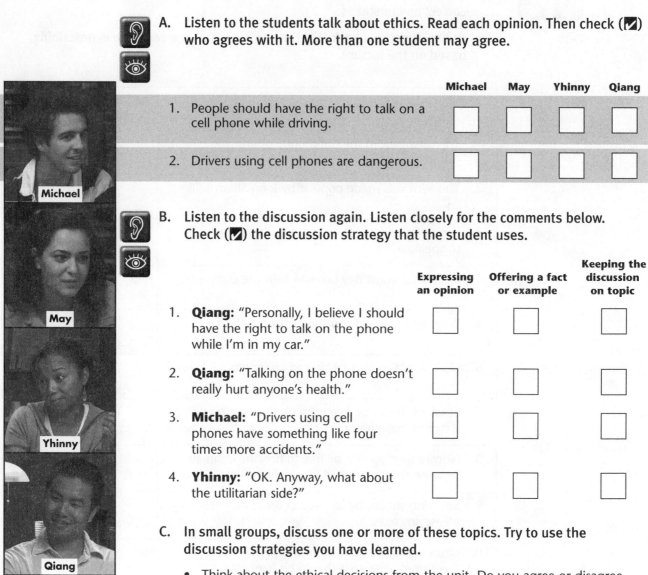

A. Listen to the students talk about ethics. Read each opinion. Then check (☑) who agrees with it. More than one student may agree.

		Michael	May	Yhinny	Qiang
1.	People should have the right to talk on a cell phone while driving.	☐	☐	☐	☐
2.	Drivers using cell phones are dangerous.	☐	☐	☐	☐

B. Listen to the discussion again. Listen closely for the comments below. Check (☑) the discussion strategy that the student uses.

		Expressing an opinion	Offering a fact or example	Keeping the discussion on topic
1.	**Qiang:** "Personally, I believe I should have the right to talk on the phone while I'm in my car."	☐	☐	☐
2.	**Qiang:** "Talking on the phone doesn't really hurt anyone's health."	☐	☐	☐
3.	**Michael:** "Drivers using cell phones have something like four times more accidents."	☐	☐	☐
4.	**Yhinny:** "OK. Anyway, what about the utilitarian side?"	☐	☐	☐

C. In small groups, discuss one or more of these topics. Try to use the discussion strategies you have learned.

- Think about the ethical decisions from the unit. Do you agree or disagree with the decisions discussed in the lecture and student discussion? Why or why not?
- Think of your own example of an ethical decision. Analyze it using the rights approach and the utilitarian approach. Which approach leads to the best decision? Why?

REVIEW *your* notes

Work with a partner. Use your notes to add details below about the two ethical approaches discussed in the lecture.

	Rights approach	Utilitarian approach
1st per. to describe this approach:		
Ex. of this approach:		
Most important thing about this approach:		
How this approach sees/ addresses public smoking:		

TAKE THE UNIT TEST

Now you are ready to take the Unit Test.

Tip!

Try adding your own examples. This can make your notes more interesting and help you better understand a new concept.

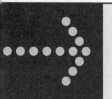

EXTEND *the* topic

You've learned about the rights and utilitarian approaches to ethical decision making. In the following activities, you'll have the chance to explore other kinds of ethical situations.

 A. **Listen to the conversation between radio personality Dr. Ethics and a caller. Then answer these questions in a small group.**

1. What is the husband's opinion about the computer? What is the woman's opinion?

2. According to Dr. Ethics, who has a right to use the computer? How does the computer help the greater good?

3. Do you agree with Dr. Ethics's opinion? Why or why not?

Some people question the ethics of driving oversized vehicles.
They say these vehicles endanger other drivers and cause
environmental problems.

B. **Discuss ethical decisions. Work individually. Think of a situation in which someone has to make an ethical decision. It can be a real situation that you have heard about or experienced, or you can create a new situation. Write a clear description of the situation. Then answer these questions.**

⸻⃕ Who is involved?

⸻⃕ Where does the situation take place?

⸻⃕ What happens?

⸻⃕ What are the possible courses of action?

C. **Meet in a small group. Take turns presenting your situation to the group. Discuss the right thing to do in each situation, and explain your reasons. Look at the problems using the rights and utilitarian approaches, if applicable.**

UNIT 12 Opportunity Cost

CONNECT *to the* topic

Economics is the study of how goods and services are traded. Economists are interested in how people interact with each other to get the things that they want and need. They're also interested in how people make choices about time, money, or other resources.

Imagine that you have two hours of free time today. You need to choose how to spend that time. If you choose one activity, you must give up doing everything else. Which activity would you choose?

Number these activities starting with 1 (your first choice) to show how you'd choose to spend your time.

____ study

____ take a nap

____ clean your house or apartment

____ visit a friend

____ go shopping

____ other: _____

Discuss your choices in a small group.

BUILD *your* vocabulary

A. The boldfaced words are from the unit lecture on opportunity cost. Listen to the sentences. Then match the words with their definitions.

____ 1. When two companies make similar products, they **compete** with each other for sales. Each company tries to sell more than the other company sells.

____ 2. Supply and demand are important **concepts** in economics. They are basic ideas that all economists need to understand.

____ 3. There are several **elements** to this problem. There are several important things we need to consider before we can figure out a solution.

     a. important parts of something
     b. to try to be better than somebody else
     c. principles or ideas

____ 4. The price tag on the car **excludes** the tax. The tax isn't included at first. It's added on when you pay for it.

____ 5. In this course, the **focus** is on how people make economic decisions. We'll look closely at how much people work, what they buy, and how much money they save.

____ 6. My company plans to **fund** a new project. As soon as we get that money, we'll start.

     a. the center of interest or attention
     b. to provide money for something
     c. leaves something out; doesn't include something

____ 7. One of my **options** is to go to college full-time. Or another possibility I could choose is to go to college part-time and get a part-time job.

____ 8. If I go away to college, I'll have to **give up** my job here.

____ 9. My parents think I should **invest** in a college education. They think putting time and money toward an education is a good investment in my future.

     a. to put money, effort, or time into something
     b. choices of things to do
     c. to stop owning or being able to do something

____ 10. Going to college will provide me with better **opportunities** in the future. For example, if I go to college, I'll have a better chance of finding a high-paying job.

____ 11. I had a meeting with my boss. The **outcome** was good because I got the raise that I wanted.

____ 12. I am a very **valuable** employee. I am very helpful to my company, so I think my boss should give me a raise.

____ 13. The professor gave us an example of a company that makes cheap **widgets**.

     a. *an effect or result*
     b. *imaginary products made by a company*
     c. *helpful or important*
     d. *chances to do something that you'd like to do*

B. ***INTERACT WITH VOCABULARY!*** **Work with a partner. Take turns saying the sentences. Notice the boldfaced words. Circle the best word to complete the sentences.**

1. I want to earn some extra money, but I don't want to **give** (up / down) my free time.

2. I need a way to get to work, so I want to **invest** (in / on) a new car.

3. They say I can't afford to fix the car if it **breaks** (up / down).

4. If I stay home tonight, I'll lose the **opportunity** (for / to) hang out with my friends.

5. I don't have much money to spend, so I'll have to exclude the **option** (to / of) going to an expensive restaurant.

6. My parents won't **put funds** (toward / from) my trip this summer, so I'll have to earn the money myself.

7. My company wants to **come** (by / out) with a new product.

8. We will have to **compete** (to / with) another company that makes a similar product.

9. The other company's product is selling like crazy, so I think it's really important that we **put money** (at / into) advertising our product.

FOCUS *your* attention

CAUSES AND EFFECTS

When giving lectures, speakers often use signal words or phrases to show causes or reasons. They also often use words or phrases to introduce effects or results.

Here are some words that you may hear to signal causes:

> **If** I go out with my friends tonight, I won't be able to study.
>
> I really need to study tonight **because** I have a test tomorrow.
>
> **Since** the test is early in the morning, I'll need to get to bed early.

Here are some words that you may hear to signal effects:

> If I don't study enough, **then** I'll feel very nervous during the test.
>
> Going to bed late **causes** me to feel sleepy in class.
>
> I really want to see my friends, **so** I'll make plans to go out with them tomorrow.

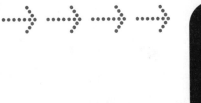

TRY IT OUT!

A. Listen to this excerpt from a lecture on economics. What signal words do you hear? What causes and effects do you hear? Complete the notes below.

B. Compare notes with a partner. What do you think the arrows (→) indicate?

<u>Advertising</u>: How much $ should a co. spend? + Which kind?

<u>cause (reason)</u>	→	<u>effect (result)</u>
e.g. run a TV commercial	→	_____
_____	→	save $, but may reach < people
_____	→	co. should start w/ research

LISTEN *to the* lecture

BEFORE YOU LISTEN

You will hear a lecture about a concept in economics called opportunity cost. Answer the following question.

How do you think the speaker will define opportunity cost?

    a.   the cost of the thing you give up to get something you want

    b.   the amount of money you pay to get what you want

    c.   the cost of all the possible choices a company has

LISTEN FOR MAIN IDEAS

A. Close your book. Listen to the lecture and take notes.

B. Use your notes. Decide if the statements below are true or false. Write *T* (true) or *F* (false). Change the false statements to make them true.

Opportunity cost is . . .

_____   1.   a way of thinking about choices.

_____   2.   only useful in making business decisions.

_____   3.   the amount of money you pay for something.

_____   4.   the most valuable thing you give up to get what you want.

_____   5.   only useful when there are two choices.

LISTEN FOR DETAILS

A. Close your book. Listen to the lecture again. Add details to your notes and correct any mistakes.

B. Use your notes. Complete these notes about the examples in the lecture.

Opportunity Cost

Ex. 1: _____ hrs. of free time

    Choices:

    _____ → won't have time to _____

    _____ → won't have time to _____

    Opportunity cost of cleaning apt. = _____

    Opportunity cost of taking a nap = _____

Ex. 2: Int'l Widgets has extra _____

    Choices: _____   OR build _____

    Opp. cost = _____   Opp. cost = _____

Add 3rd element

Ex. 3: Widgets popular → don't need to _____

    Need new _____

    Workers want _____

    Fund _____ → opp. cost _____

Ex. 4: Workers _____

    Factory starting to _____

    Other co. has _____

    → need to _____

    Fund new factory → opp. cost = _____

TALK *about the* topic

A. Listen to the students talk about opportunity cost. Read each opinion. Then check (☑) who agrees with it. More than one student may agree.

	Ayman	Molly	Rob	Alana
1. The lecture was interesting and practical.	☐	☐	☐	☐
2. The example about taking a nap versus cleaning your apartment was clearest.	☐	☐	☐	☐
3. The example about the widgets worked best.	☐	☐	☐	☐

B. Listen to the discussion again. Listen closely for the comments below. Check (☑) the discussion strategy that the student uses.

	Agreeing	Disagreeing	Keeping the discussion on topic
1. **Rob:** "Yeah, I agree."	☐	☐	☐
2. **Molly:** "Yeah, that was a great example."	☐	☐	☐
3. **Alana:** "Really? For me, the widget example worked better . . . "	☐	☐	☐
4. **Alana:** "Anyway—back to the widget example . . . "	☐	☐	☐

C. In small groups, discuss one or more of these topics. Try to use the discussion strategies you have learned.

- Which example from the lecture did you think was the most useful? How did it help you understand the concept of opportunity cost?
- Do you think that the concept of opportunity cost is useful for making decisions in your everyday life? Give an example of how you might use it to make a decision in your life.

REVIEW your notes

Read your notes. Did you write down key words and meanings? Can you explain the main ideas of the lecture? Work with a partner. Discuss and complete the notes below.

def. of opportunity cost ↓

Opportunity cost is _____

_____

Opportunity cost is not _____

_____

Ex.	Choices	The opportunity cost of . . .
(Ex. 1) 2 hours of free time		_____ is _____ .
(Ex. 2) Int'l Widgets		_____ is _____ .
(Ex. 3) Int'l Widgets • ____ product • need ____ • workers ____		_____ is _____ .
(Ex. 4) Int'l Widgets • ____ workers • old _____ • need _____		_____ is _____ .

TAKE THE UNIT TEST

Now you are ready to take the Unit Test.

Tip!

Remember: Cause is signaled by words such as *if, because,* and *since.* Effect is signaled by words such as *then, so,* and *will cause.*

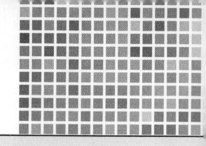

 # EXTEND *the* topic

Now that you've learned about the concept of opportunity cost, try seeing how it works in the following activities.

 A. **Listen to this blogcaster describe reaching a decision about buying a morning cup of coffee. Then answer these questions in pairs.**

1. What are the woman's choices?

2. In a week, what does she have to give up in order to get coffee?

3. According to the woman, what is the opportunity cost of getting coffee for one week?

4. What decision did the woman make? Do you think it was a good decision? Why or why not?

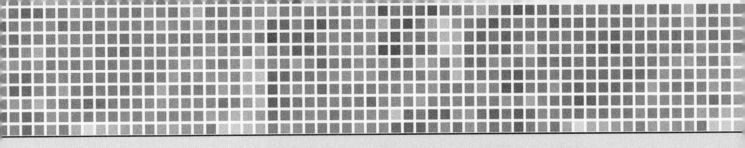

B. **Role-play making a decision. Work in a small group. Choose one of the situations below, or create your own situation.**

····⟩ A student has just graduated from high school. He has received some money as a gift. He wants to spend the money on a car and get a job. His parents want him to save the money and go to college.

····⟩ A family has three weeks to spend together this summer. They are trying to decide how to spend their time.

····⟩ Some friends have just won $5,000 in a contest. They want to spend the money together.

Discuss these questions to decide the details of your situation:

····⟩ What are the choices?

····⟩ What do the people have to give up to get what they want?

····⟩ What decision should they make?

C. **Perform a role-play for the class in which the people negotiate and decide what to do. As you watch other role-plays, listen and answer these questions.**

····⟩ What are the opportunity costs of the decision?

····⟩ Do you think they made the right decision? Why or why not?

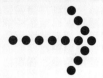

Numbers indicate the sublist of the Academic Word List. For example, *abandon* and its family members are in Sublist 8. Sublist 1 contains the most frequent words in the list, and Sublist 10 contains the least frequent. **Boldfacing** indicates that the word is taught in *Contemporary Topics 1*. The page number of the section where the word is taught is indicated in parentheses.

abandon	8	anticipate	9	bulk	9	compile	10
abstract	6	apparent	4	capable	6	complement	8
academy	5	append	8	capacity	5	complex	2
access	4	appreciate	8	**category** (p. 43)	2	component	3
accommodate	9	**approach** (p. 33)	1	cease	9	compound	5
accompany	8	appropriate	2	challenge	5	comprehensive	7
accumulate	8	approximate	4	channel	7	comprise	7
accurate	6	arbitrary	8	chapter	2	compute	2
achieve (p. 3)	2	area	1	chart	8	conceive	10
acknowledge	6	**aspect** (p. 23)	2	chemical	7	**concentrate** (p. 33)	4
acquire (p. 13)	2	assemble	10	**circumstance** (p. 33)	3	**concept** (p. 113)	1
adapt	7	assess	1	cite	6	conclude	2
adequate	4	assign	6	civil	4	concurrent	9
adjacent	10	assist	2	clarify	8	conduct	2
adjust	5	**assume** (p. 83)	1	classic	7	**confer** (p. 33)	4
administrate	2	assure	9	clause	5	confine	9
adult	7	attach	6	code	4	confirm	7
advocate	7	attain	9	coherent	9	**conflict** (p. 33)	5
affect (p. 63)	2	attitude	4	coincide	9	conform	8
aggregate	6	attribute	4	collapse	10	consent	3
aid	7	author	6	colleague	10	**consequent** (p. 23)	2
albeit	10	authority	1	commence	9	considerable	3
allocate	6	**automate** (p. 53)	8	comment	3	consist	1
alter	5	available	1	commission	2	constant	3
alternative	3	aware	5	commit	4	constitute	1
ambiguous	8	behalf	9	commodity	8	constrain	3
amend	5	**benefit** (p. 33)	1	**communicate** (p. 43)	4	**construct** (p. 53)	2
analogy	9	bias	8	**community** (p. 103)	2	consult	5
analyze	1	bond	6	compatible	9	**consume** (p. 73)	2
annual	4	brief	6	compensate	3	contact	5

contemporary	8	despite	4	ensure	3	fluctuate	8
context	1	detect	8	entity	5	**focus** (p. 113)	2
contract	1	deviate	8	**environment** (p. 13)	1	format	9
contradict	8	device	9	equate	2	formula	1
contrary	7	devote	9	equip	7	forthcoming	10
contrast	4	differentiate	7	equivalent	5	found	9
contribute	3	dimension	4	erode	9	foundation	7
controversy	9	diminish	9	error	4	framework	3
convene	3	discrete	5	establish	1	**function** (p. 23)	1
converse	9	discriminate	6	estate	6	**fund** (p. 113)	3
convert	7	displace	8	**estimate** (p. 83)	1	fundamental	5
convince	10	display	6	**ethic** (p. 103)	9	furthermore	6
cooperate	6	dispose	7	ethnic	4	gender	6
coordinate	3	distinct	2	evaluate	2	generate	5
core	3	distort	9	eventual	8	generation	5
corporate	3	distribute	1	**evident** (p. 63)	1	globe	7
correspond	3	diverse	6	evolve	5	**goal** (p. 3)	4
couple	7	document	3	exceed	6	**grade** (p. 63)	7
create (p. 43)	1	domain	6	**exclude** (p. 113)	3	grant	4
credit (p. 93)	2	domestic	4	exhibit	8	guarantee	7
criteria	3	dominate	3	expand	5	guideline	8
crucial	8	draft	5	expert	6	hence	4
culture	2	drama	8	explicit	6	hierarchy	7
currency	8	duration	9	exploit	8	highlight	8
cycle	4	dynamic	7	export	1	hypothesis	4
data (p. 3)	1	**economy** (p. 112)	1	expose	5	identical	7
debate	4	edit	6	external	5	identify	1
decade	7	**element** (p. 113)	2	extract	7	ideology	7
decline	5	eliminate	7	facilitate	5	ignorance	6
deduce	3	**emerge** (p. 43)	4	**factor** (p. 13)	1	illustrate	3
define	1	emphasis	3	feature	2	**image** (p. 43)	5
definite	7	empirical	7	federal	6	immigrate	3
demonstrate	3	enable	5	fee	6	**impact** (p. 23)	2
denote	8	encounter	10	file	7	implement	4
deny	7	energy	5	**final** (p. 93)	2	implicate	4
depress	10	enforce	5	finance	1	implicit	8
derive	1	enhance	6	finite	7	imply	3
design (p. 53)	2	enormous	10	flexible	6	impose	4

incentive	6	investigate	4	minimal	9	parallel	4
incidence	6	invoke	10	minimize	8	parameter	4
incline	10	involve	1	minimum	6	participate	2
income (p. 3)	1	isolate	7	ministry	6	partner	3
incorporate	6	**issue** (p. 63)	1	minor	3	passive	9
index	6	item	2	mode	7	perceive	2
indicate	1	**job** (p. 93)	4	**modify** (p. 73)	5	**percent** (p. 23)	1
individual (p. 103)	1	journal	2	monitor	5	**period** (p. 13)	1
induce	8	justify	3	**motive** (p. 13)	6	persist	10
inevitable	8	label	4	mutual	9	perspective	5
infer	7	labor	1	negate	3	phase	4
infrastructure	8	layer	3	network	5	phenomenon	7
inherent	9	lecture	6	neutral	6	**philosophy** (p. 103)	3
inhibit	6	legal	1	nevertheless	6	physical	3
initial	3	legislate	1	nonetheless	10	plus	8
initiate	6	levy	10	norm	9	policy	1
injure (p. 23)	2	liberal	5	**normal** (p. 73)	2	portion	9
innovate	7	license	5	notion	5	pose	10
input	6	likewise	10	notwithstanding	10	**positive** (p. 2)	2
insert	7	**link** (p. 23)	3	**nuclear** (p. 53)	8	potential	2
insight	9	**locate** (p. 83)	3	objective	5	practitioner	8
inspect	8	logic	5	**obtain** (p. 53)	2	precede	6
instance	3	maintain	2	**obvious** (p. 13)	4	precise	5
institute	2	**major** (p. 103)	1	occupy	4	predict	4
instruct	6	manipulate	8	occur	1	predominant	8
integral	9	manual	9	odd	10	preliminary	9
integrate	4	margin	5	offset	8	presume	6
integrity	10	mature	9	ongoing	10	previous	2
intelligence	6	maximize	3	**option** (p. 113)	4	**primary** (p. 73)	2
intense	8	mechanism	4	orient	5	prime	5
interact (p. 63)	3	**media** (p. 63)	7	**outcome** (p. 113)	3	principal	4
intermediate	9	mediate	9	output	4	**principle** (p. 103)	1
internal	4	medical	5	**overall** (p. 103)	4	prior	4
interpret	1	medium	9	overlap	9	priority	7
interval	6	mental	5	overseas	6	proceed	1
intervene	7	**method** (p. 3)	1	panel	10	process	1
intrinsic	10	migrate	6	paradigm	7	professional	4
invest (p. 113)	2	military	9	paragraph	8	prohibit	7

project (p. 83)	4	respond	1	stable	5	thesis	7
promote	4	restore	8	statistic	4	topic	7
proportion	3	restrain	9	status	4	trace	6
prospect	8	restrict	2	straightforward	10	**tradition** (p. 43)	2
protocol	9	**retain** (p. 73)	4	strategy	2	transfer	2
psychology (p. 2)	5	reveal	6	stress	4	transform	6
publication	7	revenue	5	structure	1	transit	5
publish	3	reverse	7	**style** (p. 43)	5	transmit	7
purchase (p. 73)	2	revise	8	submit	7	transport	6
pursue	5	revolution	9	subordinate	9	trend	5
qualitative	9	rigid	9	subsequent	4	trigger	9
quote	7	**role** (p. 13)	1	subsidy	6	ultimate	7
radical	8	route	9	substitute	5	undergo	10
random	8	scenario	9	successor	7	underlie	6
range	2	schedule	8	sufficient	3	undertake	4
ratio	5	scheme	3	sum	4	uniform	8
rational	6	scope	6	summary	4	unify	9
react	3	section	1	supplement	9	unique	7
recover	6	sector	1	survey	2	utilize	6
refine	9	secure	2	**survive** (p. 93)	7	valid	3
regime	4	seek	2	suspend	9	vary	1
region	2	select	2	sustain	5	vehicle	8
register	3	**sequence** (p. 83)	3	symbol	5	version	5
regulate	2	series	4	tape	6	via	8
reinforce	8	sex	3	target	5	violate	9
reject	5	**shift** (p. 23)	3	**task** (p. 53)	3	virtual	8
relax	9	**significant** (p. 53)	1	**team** (p. 93)	9	visible	7
release	7	similar	1	technical	3	vision	9
relevant (p. 3)	2	simulate	7	**technique** (p. 43)	3	visual	8
reluctance	10	site	2	**technology** (p. 83)	3	volume	3
rely	3	so-called	10	temporary	9	voluntary	7
remove	3	sole	7	tense	8	welfare	5
require (p. 3)	1	somewhat	7	terminate	8	whereas	5
research (p. 3)	1	**source** (p. 73)	1	text	2	whereby	10
reside	2	specific	1	theme	8	widespread	8
resolve (p. 33)	4	specify	3	**theory** (p. 13)	1		
resource	2	sphere	9	thereby	8		

APPENDIX B: affix charts

Learning the meanings of affixes can help you identify unfamiliar words that you read or hear. A *prefix* is a letter or group of letters at the beginning of a word. It usually changes the meaning. A *suffix* is a letter or group of letters at the end of a word. It usually changes the part of speech.

The charts below and on page 127 contain common prefixes and suffixes. Refer to the charts as you use this book.

Prefixes

PREFIX	MEANING	EXAMPLE
a-, ab-, il-, im-, in-, ir-, un-	not, without	atypical, abnormal, illegal, impossible, inconvenient, irregular, unfair
anti-	opposed to, against	antisocial, antiseptic
co-, col-, com-, con-, cor-	with, together	coexist, collect, commune, connect, correct
de-	give something the opposite quality	decriminalize
dis-	not, remove	disapprove, disarm
ex-	no longer, former	ex-wife, ex-president
ex-	out, from	export, exit
extra-	outside, beyond	extracurricular, extraordinary
im-, in-	in, into	import, incoming
inter-	between, among	international
post-	later than, after	postgraduate
pro-	in favor of	pro-education
semi-	half, partly	semicircle, semi-literate
sub-	under, below, less important	subway, submarine, subordinate
super-	larger, greater, stronger	supermarket, supervisor

Suffixes

SUFFIX	MEANING	EXAMPLE
-able, -ible	having the quality of, capable of (adj)	comfortable, responsible
-al, -ial	relating to (adj)	professional, ceremonial
-ance, -ence, -ancy, -ency	the act, state, or quality of (n)	performance, intelligence, conservancy, competency
-ation, -tion, -ion	the act, state, or result of (n)	examination, selection, facilitation
-ar, -er, -or, -ist	someone who does a particular thing (n)	beggar, photographer, editor, psychologist
-ful	full of (adj)	beautiful, harmful, fearful
-ify, -ize	give something a particular quality (v)	clarify, modernize
-ility	the quality of (n)	affordability, responsibility, humility
-ism	a political or religious belief system (n)	atheism, capitalism
-ist	relating to (or someone who has) a political or religious belief (adj, n)	Buddhist, socialist
-ive, -ous, -ious	having a particular quality (adj)	creative, dangerous, mysterious
-ity	a particular quality (n)	popularity, creativity
-less	without (adj)	careless, worthless
-ly	in a particular way (adj, adv)	briefly, fluently
-ment	conditions that result from something (n)	government, development
-ness	quality of (n)	happiness, seriousness

CD: tracking guide

TRACK	ACTIVITY	PAGE
CD 1		
1	Introduction	
UNIT 1		
2	Build Your Vocabulary	3
3	Try It Out!	5
4	Listen for Main Ideas and Listen for Details	6–7
5	Talk About the Topic, Parts A and B	8
6	Take the Unit Test	9
7	Extend the Topic, Part A	10
UNIT 2		
8	Build Your Vocabulary	13
9	Try It Out!	15
10	Listen for Main Ideas and Listen for Details	16–17
11	Talk About the Topic, Parts A and B	18
12	Take the Unit Test	19
13	Extend the Topic, Part A	20
UNIT 3		
14	Build Your Vocabulary	23
15	Try It Out!	25
16	Listen for Main Ideas and Listen for Details	26–27
17	Talk About the Topic, Parts A and B	28
18	Take the Unit Test	29
19	Extend the Topic, Part A	30
UNIT 4		
20	Build Your Vocabulary	33
21	Try It Out!	35
22	Listen for Main Ideas and Listen for Details	36–37
23	Talk About the Topic, Parts A and B	38
24	Take the Unit Test	39
25	Extend the Topic, Part A	40

TRACK	ACTIVITY	PAGE
CD 2		
1	Introduction	
UNIT 5		
2	Build Your Vocabulary	43
3	Try It Out!	45
4	Listen for Main Ideas and Listen for Details	46–47
5	Talk About the Topic, Parts A and B	48
6	Take the Unit Test	49
7	Extend the Topic, Part A	50
UNIT 6		
8	Build Your Vocabulary	53
9	Try It Out!	55
10	Listen for Main Ideas and Listen for Details	56–57
11	Talk About the Topic, Parts A and B	58
12	Take the Unit Test	59
13	Extend the Topic, Part A	60
UNIT 7		
14	Build Your Vocabulary	63
15	Try It Out!	65
16	Listen for Main Ideas and Listen for Details	66–67
17	Talk About the Topic, Parts A and B	68
18	Take the Unit Test	69
19	Extend the Topic, Part A	70
UNIT 8		
20	Build Your Vocabulary	73
21	Try It Out!	75
22	Listen for Main Ideas and Listen for Details	76–77
23	Talk About the Topic, Parts A and B	78
24	Take the Unit Test	79
25	Extend the Topic, Part A	80

TRACK	ACTIVITY	PAGE
CD 3		
1	Introduction	
UNIT 9		
2	Build Your Vocabulary	83
3	Try It Out!	85
4	Listen for Main Ideas and Listen for Details	86–87
5	Talk About the Topic, Parts A and B	88
6	Take the Unit Test	89
7	Extend the Topic, Part A	90
UNIT 10		
8	Build Your Vocabulary	93
9	Try It Out!	95
10	Listen for Main Ideas and Listen for Details	96–97
11	Talk About the Topic, Parts A and B	98
12	Take the Unit Test	99
13	Extend the Topic, Part A	100
UNIT 11		
14	Build Your Vocabulary	103
15	Try It Out!	105
16	Listen for Main Ideas and Listen for Details	106–107
17	Talk About the Topic, Parts A and B	108
18	Take the Unit Test	109
19	Extend the Topic, Part A	110
UNIT 12		
20	Build Your Vocabulary	113
21	Try It Out!	115
22	Listen for Main Ideas and Listen for Details	116–117
23	Talk About the Topic, Parts A and B	118
24	Take the Unit Test	119
25	Extend the Topic, Part A	120

DVD: tracking guide

UNIT	FEATURE	STUDENT BOOK ACTIVITY
1	Lecture Coaching Tips Presentation Points Student Discussion	Listen for Main Ideas and Listen for Details, pages 6–7 Talk About the Topic, Parts A and B, page 68
2	Lecture Coaching Tips Presentation Points Student Discussion	Listen for Main Ideas and Listen for Details, pages 16–17 Talk About the Topic, Parts A and B, page 18
3	Lecture Coaching Tips Presentation Points Student Discussion	Listen for Main Ideas and Listen for Details, pages 26–27 Talk About the Topic, Parts A and B, page 28
4	Lecture Coaching Tips Presentation Points Student Discussion	Listen for Main Ideas and Listen for Details, pages 36–37 Talk About the Topic, Parts A and B, page 38
5	Lecture Coaching Tips Presentation Points Student Discussion	Listen for Main Ideas and Listen for Details, pages 46–47 Talk About the Topic, Parts A and B, page 48
6	Lecture Coaching Tips Presentation Points Student Discussion	Listen for Main Ideas and Listen for Details, pages 56–57 Talk About the Topic, Parts A and B, page 58
7	Lecture Coaching Tips Presentation Points Student Discussion	Listen for Main Ideas and Listen for Details, pages 66–67 Talk About the Topic, Parts A and B, page 68

UNIT	FEATURE	STUDENT BOOK ACTIVITY
8	Lecture Coaching Tips Presentation Points	Listen for Main Ideas and Listen for Details, pages 76–77
	Student Discussion	Talk About the Topic, Parts A and B, page 78
9	Lecture Coaching Tips Presentation Points	Listen for Main Ideas and Listen for Details, pages 86–87
	Student Discussion	Talk About the Topic, Parts A and B, page 88
10	Lecture Coaching Tips Presentation Points	Listen for Main Ideas and Listen for Details, pages 96–97
	Student Discussion	Talk About the Topic, Parts A and B, page 98
11	Lecture Coaching Tips Presentation Points	Listen for Main Ideas and Listen for Details, pages 106–107
	Student Discussion	Talk About the Topic, Parts A and B, page 108
12	Lecture Coaching Tips Presentation Points	Listen for Main Ideas and Listen for Details, pages 116–117
	Student Discussion	Talk About the Topic, Parts A and B, page 118

credits

Photo Credits: Page 2 (left) Shutterstock.com, (right) © Gregg Segal/Getty Images/Stone, (bottom) Fotolia.com; **Page 4** Image Source/SuperStock; **Page 6** Shutterstock; **Page 7** Digital Vision/Alamy; **Page 12** Shutterstock; **Page 17** Shutterstock; **Page 20** Shutterstock; **Page 21** © Ken Seet/Corbis; **Page 30** Shutterstock; **Page 31** © David Hanover/Getty Images/Stone; **Page 32** (left) Shutterstock, (center) Spencer Platt/Getty Images, (right) Shutterstock; **Page 37** Shutterstock; **Page 40** (left) © Corbis, (right) © Corbis; **Page 42** Accession number: 1998.109 Artist: Shiraga, Kazuo Title: *Untitled* Date: 1959 Medium: Oil on Canvas Dimensions: 70 7/8 × 110 in. Collection Walker Art Center, Minneapolis, T.B. Walker Acquisition Fund, 1998; **Page 43** (left) Francois Guillot/Getty Images; **Page 43** (right) Lebrecht Music and Arts Photo Library/Alamy; **Page 44** © Bettmann/Corbis; **Page 46** (left) Bridgeman-Giraudon/Art Resource, NY; (center)Réunion des Musées Nationaux/Art Resource, NY; (right) CNAC/MNAM/ Dist. Réunion des Musées Nationaux/Art Resource, NY; **Page 47** Getty Images **Page 50** © Alfredo Aldai/epa/Corbis; **Page 52** (left) NASA, (center) AP Photo/ Shizuo Kambayashi, (right) Douglas McFadd/Getty Images, (lower left) Glow Images/SuperStock, (lower right) Getty Images; **Page 53** © Rykoff Collection/ Corbis; **Page 56** NASA, © Hrvoje Polan/Getty, © Glow Images/SuperStock, Erik Möller, © Andy Rain/epa/Corbis, ©Hulton Archive/Getty Images; **Page 62** (left) Shutterstock, (center) © Kristy-Anne Glubish/Design Pics/Corbis, (right) © Reed Kaestner/Corbis; **Page 66** Shutterstock; **Page 67** Shutterstock; **Page 70** Shutterstock; **Page 71** © Jose Luis Pelaez Inc./Corbis; **Page 73** Shutterstock; **Page 74** © Reuters/ Corbis; **Page 76** Shutterstock, © Doug Wilson/Corbis, © Skip Nall/Getty Images/Photodisc; **Page 77** Shutterstock; **Page 82** Shutterstock; **Page 86** Shutterstock; **Page 91** Courtesy of NASA; **Page 92** (left) © Hulton-Deutsch Collection/Corbis, (center) Underwood & Underwood/Corbis, (right) Michael Nichols/Getty Images; **Page 100** NASA; **Page 102** Richard Hutchings; **Page 110** © Hemera Technologies/Ablestock/Jupiterimages Corporation; **Page 111** Shutterstock; **Page 112** (left) Karin Dreyer/Getty Images; (center) Blend Images/SuperStock; (right) OJO Images/SuperStock; **Page 120** Shutterstock

Text Credits: Page 10 survey adapted from survey by Martin Seligman, University of Pennsylvania; **Page 50** audio interview inspired by *www.gallerydir.com/ art-web/COMMUNITY/data/LINK/ARTICLES/NAME/ABSTRACT_ART;* **Page 80** Survey inspired by the Pew Initiative on Food and Biology, Web site: www.pewtrusts.org/uploadedFiles/wwwpewtrustsorg/Public_Opinion/Food_and_ Biotechnology/2006summary.pdf

These are the **discussion strategies** that you will hear the students in the Student Discussion videos using. Consider starting a list of the expressions you learn for each one.

- Asking for opinions or ideas
- Expressing an opinion
- Agreeing
- Disagreeing
- Offering a fact or example
- Asking for clarification or confirmation
- Keeping the discussion on topic
- Paraphrasing
- Trying to reach a consensus